Countdown to Retirement

Designing Your Financial Future

Kevin H. Myeroff
& the Staff of
NCA Financial Planners

MEISTER PRESS

Charleston, South Carolina, USA

Requests for permission to reprint portions of this book, or to obtain a
copy of this book, may be directed to:

NCA Financial Planners
6449 Wilson Mills Rd., Cleveland, OH 44143 USA
Telephone: 440/473-1115 FAX: 440/473-0186
Web site: <http://www.ncafinancial.com>

Published by:

Meister Press, Duncan Jaenicke, President
PO Box 1296 / Goose Creek, SC 29445 USA
Phone: 843/873-8703 FAX: 843/873-8703
E-mail: dunkmeister@sc.rr.com / Web site: <www.dunkmeister.com>

Library of Congress Cataloging-in-Publication Data

Myeroff, Kevin H.
Countdown to Retirement--Designing Your Financial
Future / Kevin H. Myeroff
p. cm.
(Bibliographical references available upon request).
ISBN 0-9643136-6-9
1. Personal Finance. 2. Retirement. 3. Investments. I. Title.

Printed in the United States of America

DEDICATION

In writing this dedication, I struggled as I considered several groups of people, from which I was going to pick one group to honor. Then I thought, *Why not honor all of them?* So I will.

To the dedicated support staff of NCA Financial Planners, people who work behind the scenes to ensure the highest quality of service to our clients.

To the most talented group of financial planners, paraplanners and financial planning assistants on the planet. You are dedicated to making decisions and recommendations with only one thought in mind: what is best for our clients. You have my respect, and more importantly, the respect of our customers.

Perhaps most importantly, to the spouses, children and 'significant others' of our professional staff. You often must put up with the long hours, weekend meetings, and travel that are part and parcel of a service business. We love you dearly; your indirect contribution to the well-being of our clients yields untold benefits for countless retirees and future retirees.

CONTENTS

ACKNOWLEDGMENTS

Several of our clients consented to be interviewed for background material for this book; we are indebted to them. As they used to say on "Dragnet," the names have been changed to protect the innocent!

We would also like to acknowledge you, the reader of this book, since the future belongs to those who prepare for it.

Last but not least, thanks to our editor and producer, Duncan Jaenicke ('The DunkMeister'), who often had to deal with 'too many cooks in the kitchen.'

INTRODUCTION

Most people walk into our financial planning office with knots in their stomachs. Subconsciously, they know the 'countdown to retirement' clock is already ticking, and they're worried that they may mess it up.

Let's face it. Most folks, regardless of income level, are pretty much lost when it comes to understanding *when* they can retire, *how* they can retire, or even *if it will be possible* for them to retire.

As you might imagine, this is a highly emotional topic; for many it is charged with fear, frustration, and anxiety. Although the idea of planning your retirement may carry the scent of highly technical formulas, confusing numbers, high-flying economic theories, and high-pressure stockbrokers, in reality it doesn't have to be scary at all. We believe that, by consulting the right resources and knowing what questions to ask of whom, this fairly frightening process can be quite palatable indeed. That's what this book is all about.

We've counseled thousands of clients who felt just like you. We've helped millionaires secure their estates for the next generation, who were in danger of losing a major chunk of it to the tax collector. On the other end of the scale, we've helped people who were living paycheck to paycheck reorganize their financial lives and stake out a pretty decent retirement lifestyle. Our journey through the technical highways and byways of retirement planning has broadened our vision. Our experience with the emotional issues of real people—from princes to virtual paupers—has sharpened our focus.

We know what you're thinking.

We know what you're feeling.

We understand your questions, and we're alert to the issues behind your concerns. That's why we have written this book. Your peace of mind is at stake. And more importantly, your family is counting on you!

The good news is, you needn't sweat this most important of tasks. You simply need to learn the basics, put together a team of experts who can help you formulate your game plan, and then *relax*—and enjoy the ride.

Changes in Latitude, Changes in Attitude

People used to retire at age 65 with a life expectancy of age 71. Thus the assets they accumulated during their working years only needed to last through six years of retirement. Today, things have changed—people want to retire earlier, and they live longer. For example, if a person retires at age 60 and lives until age 85, he has 25 years of retirement to plan for, not six. This is a huge planning issue, a major shift from the past. Also, women on average live seven to eight years longer than men. Instead of cutting back spending so couples can "leave the kids something," retired people with money are buying a place on the beach with four bedrooms and inviting all the kids and grandkids down for a holiday. Retirees are enjoying their money *now* instead of leaving it for their offspring.

In 'the olden days,' before 1985, the goal of most of our clients was to accumulate enough money to enable them to live off their interest income without touching the nest egg itself (technically called 'the principal'). There was a preservationist mentality that said, 'Don't touch the golden goose, just live off its earnings.' This line of thinking may have come from our parents or grandparents, folks who survived the Great Depression, who always wanted to maximize savings and thereby be prepared for *any* disaster that might rear its ugly head.

Today, however, things have changed. The vast majority of our clients expect to benefit from more than their interest earnings alone. And while they would like to leave their children an inheritance, if possible, they don't want to sacrifice an enjoyable standard of living to guarantee that it will happen.

The preservation-at-any-cost instinct is gone. Today's retirees have a different focus: Most just want their money to last as long as their lives do.

The old expression 'Time marches on' is truer than ever. You may be reading this book and only be in your 20s or 30s, or you may be middle-aged in your 40s or 50s. Or you might have achieved 60-plus years and be on the verge of retirement. And, just like when you had little kids and took that long drive to Grandma's house with your children whining, "Are we there yet?", you wonder, somewhere in the back of your mind: *How close to the finish line am I, anyway?*

Good question. Knowing where you stand is certainly the first step to moving forward.

These days, your retirement age isn't as fixed as it once was. That 'magic age' of 65 doesn't neces-sarily represent a hard-and-fast milepost anymore; more people want to retire early, in their 50s, or even earlier, in their late 40s. Others reject the full-time "gone fishin'" retirement lifestyle and want to simply scale back their work lives at a certain age or volun-teer their efforts at their church, synagogue, or civic organization.

Regardless of which avenue you choose for retirement, our point is this: you need to know, wher-ever you are today along that timeline, how close—or how *possible*—your retirement is.

Is it within reach, or not? A host of other ques-tions comes to mind, thoughts that race through your head and heart, begging for answers:

❖ Will you be able to afford to travel, as you've

always dreamed, or will you be using food stamps at the supermarket to survive?

❖ Can you move to Florida and live on a golf course, or will finances keep you stuck in Siberia?

❖ Will you have to depend on your adult children for long-term care if your health should fail gradually, or can you pay for health care yourself?

❖ Will you be able to live comfortably if your spouse dies before you?

❖ Will Social Security even be there at all when you arrive at retirement, and if so, what level of income is reasonable to expect from it?

❖ What effect will various interest-rate scenarios over the next 20 years have on your ability to retire in the lifestyle to which you've become accustomed?

Job One, as the Ford ads used to say, is to take a brutally honest look at your present financial situation (a daunting task, without outside professional help) and determine what changes, if any, you need to make *today* to make your tomorrows happy, healthy, and fulfilling.

That's where this book comes in; along the way, we'll educate you so you can understand the overall process. Because even though you need experts on your retirement team, you as the consumer of this advice need to understand the basics in order to evaluate the quality of the advice you're getting.

By accurately taking your financial 'vital signs' now, you'll have an accurate foundation on which to build your plan. If you're on your way to achieving retirement on schedule, you want to know that. But if you're not doing well and are way off track, you surely want to know that, too, so you can take corrective action to avoid a rude awakening down the road. Sure, fast-food restaurants love to hire seniors, but who wants to be flipping burgers in your golden years?

The stakes are high, but you can feel confident now that you've got this book in your hands. Here you have a wealth of information—literally at your fingertips—that will help assure that your golden years truly *are* golden, in a financial sense and in many other ways. While happiness in retirement involves more than merely dollars and cents, having sufficient financial resources opens up practically unlimited horizons for enjoying the final innings of this game called life.

A little 'housekeeping' item, before we turn you loose to enjoy these pages: Any generic pronoun reference in this book applies equally to both genders.

We're pleased that you've decided to invest some of your time reading our thoughts and working on the solutions you need for the future. We're confident that the thoughts, tools, and strategies contained in these pages will enhance your life—both now and

in the days and years to come.
        Let's get started.

CHAPTER 1

Survey the Landscape: Gathering Your Data

S tuff. Most of us acquire lots and lots of stuff as we careen through life in the fast lane. But for our purposes here, we need to be more specific about this convenient catch-all phrase. We need to divide all your stuff into two categories: *assets* and *liabilities.*

As opposed to the traditional accounting definition, we are going to look at assets from a retirement and cash flow point of view. Assets are things that bring you income, whether now (e.g., a business you might own) or in the future (e.g., that pile of diamonds in your safe-deposit box, or a company pension plan). In contrast, liabilities are things that don't bring you income; they cost you—whether now (e.g., that home mortgage you pay on each month) or in the future (e.g., your children's or grandchildren's college education).

So get out a legal pad, or your diary, or your computer—anything to help you tally up your stuff. And, as obvious as this might seem, *write it all down.* Many people seem to think that flying by the seat of their pants about assets and liabilities is okay; you know, just listing off the top of your head various possessions and loans, and thinking, *That'll do it.* No—for retirement planning we need to be organized and honest and comprehensive.

Tally up everything you can think of in these two categories; if in doubt, go ahead and include an item you're not completely sure about. You can always correct this list later, when you sit down with your financial advisor. Plus, he or she may be able to help you think of other assets and liabilities that hadn't occurred to you.

Common Misconceptions About Retirement Assets

Many folks think that anything they paid money for is an asset. Wrong! For retirement planning purposes, if it doesn't produce income, it doesn't go on the asset list.

Think about it. Your house doesn't produce income. Your automobiles don't, either. Neither do your top-of-the-line golf clubs or that rare stamp collection you are planning to pass on to your grandson.

Grandma's sterling silver tea service is lovely, but it doesn't produce income sitting in the dining room. Even your prized red Corvette isn't an asset unless you plan on selling it (heaven forbid!). Usually, people's biggest assets are in their retirement accounts, such as a 401(k) plan, a profit-sharing plan, or a pension plan. Next in line would be stocks, bonds, and mutual funds.

And when you're gathering this data, do yourself a favor. When you write it down, detail it. Don't just write, "$40,000 in mutual funds." List each fund separately, because you're going to sit down later and work on this with your financial advisor, and you won't remember where your total numbers came from. From the start, make your resources as clear as possible.

If you're having trouble remembering some of your assets, you might want to go to your latest tax return and look at Schedule B, which lists all the interest and dividends received from investments. That is a good way to double-check to make sure you don't miss anything. Don't forget assets that may not appear on your tax return, such as annuities or cash value life insurance.

If you are listing investment assets from brokerage statements, remember that lots of companies only send statements quarterly, so you might not have the latest statement you need. In that case, you can call your brokerage house for a current summary of the value of your investments, or just use your last quarter's statement for now, and then update your figures at the end of the period when the statement arrives.

Keep in mind that when planning for the future, you need to take inflation into account as you consider assets; your financial advisor can help you calculate the future value of your various assets. And, as best as you can, you need to allow for unforeseen events that might affect your assets, especially if you have all your eggs in one basket, such as the stock of the company you have worked at for the last 25 years.

Listing Your Liabilities

The next step in the gathering process is to list your liabilities and the corresponding payments. Here again, detail is your friend.

You have two classes of liabilities: long- and short-term. Long-term obligations are things like a home mortgage, home equity loan, or supporting your aging parents in a nursing home for the remainder of their lives. When you list long-term liabilities such as your mortgage, detail your payments. For example, a $1,500 monthly mortgage payment might actually be the sum of three sub-parts: $1,100 for repaying the loan, $300 for property taxes, and $100 for insurance.

List short-term liabilities, such as credit card debt and auto loans. Make sure you list your balance, the monthly payments you are making, and the current interest rate you're paying on each loan.

Try to include all the possible life scenarios that could impact you as a couple or as an individual.

Perhaps you have future liabilities, such as a disabled child who will not be able to care for himself when he becomes an adult. Or maybe you foresee a potential move across the country to be near grandchildren or to get out of the ice and snow. Write down everything that may affect your financial situation over the next five to 10 years.

Honesty is the best policy; you have nothing to gain by hiding some liabilities under the rug. If you do that, the rug may look pretty lumpy by retirement time, and then it might be too late to straighten it out! Here is a sample worksheet:

			Initial	Current	Min.	Int.
Creditor	**Date**	**Purpose**	**Amt.**	**Balance**	**Pymt.**	**Rate**
1st Bank	6/4/94	Home improv.	$30,000	$22,422	$304	9%
Visa	Various	Various	$ 4,500	$ 4,000	$120	18%
2nd Bank	6/15/98	Auto loan	$15,000	$ 8,872	$562	10%
Marina	8/13/99	Boat loan	$12,000	$ 7,097	$449	12%

Liabilities Worksheet (sample)

List Your Spending/Cash Flow

Once you have listed your assets and liabilities, make a list of where your cash goes each month. If you are paying your bills on the computer, you can figure this out easily; most software packages can spit out a report of expenses for a specified time period. If you don't use a computer, go to your checkbook. Visit each check written and note a category of spending on the left side of the page. You'll want to list such categories as housing, entertainment, clothing, car, food, utilities, etc.

Next, on a separate piece of paper, list three months' worth of checks, detailing the amount you spent in each category. Multiply these numbers by four and you'll get an account of an entire year's cash flow divided into useful categories. You will easily see where your money has gone! As you do this, take more expensive months into account, adding separately such things as college tuition paid in August, vacation expenses in July, and holiday expenses in December. You'll see a sample worksheet on page 25; look it over before reading further.

These numbers are important because they get the data down in black and white. This process may be an eye-opening experience for you, as it has been for so many others. We have people come in and tell us matter-of-factly what their expenses are. Then we look at their income and calculate that they are saving $1,000 per month. We ask them how long they have been saving $1,000 per month? "Five years," they reply, so we expect to see a savings account of at least $60,000. Yet when we look at their assets, they have only $4,000 in savings.

When we ask about where the money goes, the clients may say, "Well, we guess we spend maybe $200 a month eating out."

In further discussion, the clients indicate they eat out three times per week at a cost of, say, $50 per visit. Simple math shows that they are actually spending $150 per week or $600 per month on dining out. Numbers don't lie.

This is why it's important to be honest. You're doing this for yourself. You have nobody to impress. You've got to make an honest effort to get the right answers. You may believe you've been saving $1,000 a month, but when you look in your savings account, you see $4,000. Confusion results because of the big difference between "savings" and "deferred spending." You may be putting $1,000 into a savings account each month, but if you go to the bank weeks later, take it out and spend it, that's called deferred spending. It's not true savings.

So, look for discrepancies between *perception* and *reality* when it comes to spending behavior, because they can be quite different. Shockingly so. We're not saying it's necessarily bad to eat out 12 times per month; the point here is, you have to account for what *really* happens with your pocketbook, not what you *think* happens.

List Your Hidden Assets

Next, you need to list your *hidden* assets. These are items that are not income-producing, but could yield an amount of money if needed. Hidden assets are those things you hope you will never have to use. Think about what they are and the possibilities of turning them into cash if necessary.

Under some circumstances, this may include your house. For example, if you find that you don't

Current Cash Flow Worksheet (sample)

CATEGORIES (more categories to be added as needed) >>>

Date	Check#	Payee	Amt.	Housing	Food	Insurance	ATM	Utils.	Car	Total
1/18/XX	1203	First Bank	$750	$750						$750
1/19/XX	1204	Electric Co.	$ 95					$95		$ 95
1/22/XX	n/a	Cash	$200				$200			$200
2/5/XX	1205	Mr. Grocery	$145		$145					$145
3/7/XX	1206	AllRisk	$100			$100				$100
	<<<<< (etc.) >>>>>									
Totals >>>>>>>			$1,290	$750	$145	$100	$200	$95	$0	$1,290

(note that the total of checks written [$1,290] must match the total of category expenditures [$1,290])

have enough money to retire when you want to, it may make sense to sell your house and move into a more economical apartment. Smaller quarters might even be a blessing to you as you near retirement; if the kids have moved out, you and your spouse don't need all that space, and heating and cooling costs are less painful, too. Plus, it's easier to clean an apartment than it is a two-story, four-bedroom, three-bath house. You could invest the money you earn from the house sale, along with the amount you will save in monthly payments. Since part of owning a home is paying property taxes, and some neighborhoods or counties have higher taxes or insurance rates, consider this when you are thinking about lifestyle savings. Even though such a strategy is not common, if it helps you achieve your goal of retirement by a certain age, or helps you retire instead of flipping burgers until you die, it's worth it!

Automobiles may be another hidden asset. If you have two, but in retirement will need only one, you might sell the second and invest the proceeds. Plus you could save all that money you used to spend on gasoline, oil, maintenance, snow tires, towing, and insurance.

How else might you make money in a pinch? You may have hoped to give a treasured coin collection to a grandchild, but if you need money fast, you can sell it.

As far as potential inheritances go, our best advice is to not even list them. Possible exceptions to this rule might include inheritances that have already been put away in a trust for you, *and* you know the time frame within which you're going to get the money.

There is a great TV commercial for an investment company. It shows a couple in their 70s strolling along with their 50-ish son. The father says, "Son, we need to talk to you about your inheritance."

The son says, "Yes, Dad?" The son has this hopeful look on his face. Finally, after all these years, his father is bringing up the taboo subject.

"You're not getting any," says the father.

The crestfallen look on the son's face tells the story. We're guessing that the son's retirement plan was his expected inheritance!

The mother twists the knife in this over-the-top spoof, saying, "You've been a lousy son. You didn't call me on my birthday last year. The inheritance is going to your brother—and to charities."

Crystal-ball-gazing is an inexact science at best. You can't count on your aging parents for your retirement. If they do bless you with an inheritance someday, fine; it's icing on the cake. Your efforts today and henceforth have to assume that you won't get any of that icing. And if you get a pleasant surprise, fine; but if not, you won't be on welfare in your old age. Better to have a nice surprise instead of a rude awakening.

So, don't chase that little inheritance dream. Don't even go there. You must always plan for the worst-case scenario. Better to over-prepare for retirement than to under-prepare. For example, we like to assume that a client doesn't have to earn more than an 8% or 9% return on his investments in order to achieve his goals.

Recently we sat down with a 58-year-old woman who, even at a 10% return, was not going to make it through retirement, should she live her average life expectancy. We looked at her non-income-producing assets. She had a $300,000 house with no mortgage, so we suggested she sell it and buy a $100,000 condo.

"If we invest the difference of $200,000," we told her, "you're going to be able to have sufficient funds for retirement." We made her picture rosy, because her fear of running out of money was greater than the ego loss of having to move to a smaller home. It was a no-brainer. She struggled at first to accept this strategy, but after awhile it began to grow on her, especially when she began to enjoy the feeling of being confident about her retirement, instead of fearful. Confidence in your financial planning can really make your outlook more cheerful. And this woman really liked letting the condo association cut the lawn instead of having to do it herself, so it was a blessing in many ways.

Make a Spending Plan

Last in the data-gathering process: Come up with a *spending plan*. We don't like the word "budget" because it has negative, restrictive connotations of not being *able* to spend. That's no fun. But the term "spending plan" appeals to the positive part of your mind. It lets you decide before you hit the stores how you are going to spend your money.

You already have an idea of how much you are currently living on, based on the exercise you did with your checkbook or computer. Now comes the tricky part: you need to figure out how your present expense level will compare to what you can afford in retirement. It's a complex process that we'll go into later—and it especially illustrates why you may need a financial advisor to help you plan—but for now, let's just say that chances are, your retirement living expenses may need to be different from those of your working years.

This may mean a lifestyle change. Most folks wind up having to cut back some in retirement, but it's not set in stone. Some folks, through clever planning and disciplined saving and investment habits, are lucky enough to be able to improve their standard of living in retirement. However, most folks aren't that lucky, so our goal for most people is to at least minimize the cutbacks. The good news is—and this is essentially the core message of our book—*if you start early enough and are willing to make some changes as your financial advisor may suggest*, you may even be able to *avoid* the cutbacks.

Hey—you never can tell the future with absolute certainty, but you sure can stack the deck as much as possible in your favor! That's our goal for you. We can't promise you'll wind up a millionaire in your retirement, but we're absolutely confident that we can give you the advice you need—advice that, if followed, will give you the best chance on the planet to have more than enough for your golden years.

This gathering of information is the most time-consuming and most labor-intensive part of the retirement planning process. But it's vital.

Everything that comes out of this process is a result of what goes in. If you put garbage in, you get garbage out, so it's important to get to work in a comprehensive way. The more honest and accurate you are in this stage, the more confidence you'll have in the later stages, and the better chance you'll have of achieving your goals for a wonderful retirement.

CHAPTER 2

So What?
Analyzing Your Data

L et us throw up a friendly little roadblock for you at this stage of the game.

It may be tempting to go ahead and just read through this chapter—and the rest of the book—before you do the work required in Chapter One. But if you don't do the crucial foundation work, you'll enjoy far fewer benefits. So don't cut corners. You may have thousands of dollars to gain by tracking down that last IRA statement, or you may discover that you're wasting money in unneeded insurance, or in some other place. But you won't know anything until you do the gathering work of compiling the data.

So lay this book down a moment. Go finish gathering the information you need and hurry back!

Of course, the absolute best way to interpret your data is to sit down with your financial advisor and let him help you sort it out and make some sense of it all. But in the meantime, you can get a rough idea of where you're headed by using the interactive retirement planner on our web site:

<www.ncafinancial.com>.

There, you can begin to plug your personal financial information into the formulas, questionnaires, etc. and begin the long process of arriving at answers to the key questions you must ask yourself, namely:

❖ Do I have enough money to retire?

❖ Will I be able to retire early, or at age 65, age 75, or never?

❖ Will I have to change my lifestyle in retirement?

❖ Am I on schedule, behind, or ahead of the game, regarding retirement?

Of course, the basic concept is that in retirement you don't want to run out of money before you run out of time. There are many factors involved in this calculation, some of which are:

❖ How long will you live? Will you live longer

than the average life expectancy?

❖ What kind of lifestyle do you expect in retirement?

❖ How much money do you have socked away now?

❖ How many more years do you want to work? This answer depends on how old you are now, what your health is now, at what age you want to coach Little League full time, etc.

❖ How conservative or aggressive do you have to be with your investments between now and retirement—and after retirement? If you take higher risks, your retirement fund could grow faster than average, but it also could shrink; it's a two-edged sword. Conversely, if you take lower degrees of risk, your nest egg will surely grow less, but the danger factor is a lot lower, too; you sleep better at night.

❖ What tax bracket are you in now, and which one will you be in after retirement?

...and there are a host of other factors. That's why having an experienced financial advisor at your side is so crucial. For example, the following case study involves one of our clients, Bill, who had worked for a large corporation for many years, and when it came time to plan his retirement, Bill realized he needed some help. Here's how Bill benefited from teaming up with a retirement planning specialist.

"Susan and I are the same age, 69. Back in 1990, at age 59, we attended a financial seminar which met weekly for three weeks. We were impressed by the presentation.

"Susan and I had worked for the same employer—a defense contractor—for many years: she for 23 years under various ownerships, and I for almost 10 years. I worked in data processing, eventually ending up as the manager of that area; Susan worked in various departments as an administrator. We both had 401(k)s going, but we had no real idea if they would be sufficient for our retirement needs. We knew we were approaching 65, the traditional retirement age, so we were naturally trying to get a handle on this important question. We hoped that we might be able to retire sometime in the next five or six years, but we weren't sure. As it turned out, we *were* able to retire before age 65, and in 1993, at age 62, we quit our jobs and achieved the honored status of professional loafers!

"Working with our financial advisor gives us an edge, we feel, over doing it ourselves by merely reading books and magazine articles on how to invest. For example, we often get helpful 'inside information' [the good kind of insider information, not *insider trading*, which is illegal] from our financial advisor, such as the time he told us that a certain mutual fund investment manager had left the fund and gone elsewhere. We owned quite a few shares of that fund, and it had done well under that manager's leadership. But just to be safe, our advisor suggested that we sell those shares and move to a strong alternate fund. We took his advice and have been happy with the result. This kind of inside information, though technically public information, is the kind of stuff we could never hope to pick up on as retired persons on our own, no matter how much of the trade press we might read. Besides, who wants to read investing magazines all day long, anyway? I'd rather be out volunteering with the Boy Scouts or the Red Cross or in my back yard, gardening!

"It's nice to know that there are financial pros who will pick up these industry tidbits and act upon them for our benefit. The fact that our financial advisor is independent from the funds we invest in is key, too. We get junk mail all the time from large investment firms, and I'm sure they're ethical and all that. But if they lose a key fund manager, I don't think they're going to call us, like our advisor did, and give us the advice to switch funds. No way! For my money, I want an independent voice in my ear.

"In fall 1997, our financial professional put together a 20-year plan for us to use as a guideline for what we could safely withdraw each month, each year, for the rest of our lives, or at least until we hit 87. If we make that age, I guess we'll hobble in for another 20-year plan! We like having that plan as a baseline. Of course the earnings are all projected, so it can't be totally accurate, but it gives us something to judge our progress by, year by year. No one can predict what interest rates will be in the future, or for that matter what tax hikes or cuts our government may enact. Nor can they know what the market will do—whether it will double, triple, or melt down. But at least we have a road map to see where we're at during any period.

"We're not rich by any means, but we like the increase we've seen in our nest egg under our advisor's stewardship. When we first retired in 1993, our portfolio was probably valued in the $500,000-$600,000 range. Today, some seven years later, our total valuation is probably $1,000,000-$1,100,000, and that includes our having drawn a decent retirement income out of it for those seven years! So we're as pleased as we can be.

"We have two grown children, daughters, who both have families of their own. We have seven grandchildren between them. Our sons-in-law are fine men, and our daughters aren't counting on any huge inheritance when we pass away. They are taking responsibility for their own futures, which is as it should be. And it's a good thing, since our 20-year plan shows our nest egg going down to zero at the end of the year 2017!

"Of course, if we both die earlier than the plan projects, there may be some estate to pass along to them, but that would be 'icing on the cake.' If some of our investments do better than the plan predicts that they will, we could have funds available to us beyond 2017.

"Now, if we're both still going strong at age

89, we can adjust our expenses accordingly beforehand, so we're not really worried about the plan showing our cash running out in 20 years. We probably won't need two cars by then, so that'd save some money each month. And we could sell our big house and downsize, so that would free up some capital. Or we could take out a reverse mortgage, or any of a host of other coping mechanisms that our advisor has taught us. So it's not that our life will come crashing to a halt if we're still above the sod in 20 years. The plan just gives us a tremendous tool to gauge our decisions by, as time marches on."

* * * * *

Let's go back to the interactive retirement planner on our web site. If you haven't done so already, spend some time plugging your numbers into that tool. If you don't know what the various amounts are, just make your best estimate. You're going to sharpen this information later, when you sit down with your financial advisor, so don't worry about being perfectly accurate at this stage. The web site planner is for getting into the ballpark; the professional is for the precision you'll need eventually.

Educating yourself on the basics of retirement planning is sort of like paying close attention to your own health, watching for symptoms and analyzing how you feel. But when you go for your annual checkup, the doctor has diagnostic tools available to pinpoint your exact ailments. He may confirm the fact that everything will be all right if you follow general guidelines. He'll point out things you need to know to sustain your health. The doctor's job is to maximize your peace of mind and to care for the crucial technical details that he went to school to learn; so it is with your financial advisor.

Where Are You in the Countdown to Retirement?

For our purposes in this book, we'll discuss three possible outcomes of this financial analysis you'll do roughly by yourself and then precisely with your financial advisor. At this stage in your life, you'll find yourself in one of these three categories:

❖ On Schedule
❖ Behind Schedule
❖ Ahead of Schedule

In other words, if your ideal retirement would be to retire at age 63 with $50,000 per year in after-tax income, are you on-target to hit that goal, or not? And if not, what must you do to catch up?

Now each of these three scenarios comes with its own attendant set of emotions. If you are on schedule or ahead of schedule, you might be elated. If you're behind schedule, you might be a little nervous—or downright depressed!

Our best advice for you, when you get a preliminary reading on your situation, is: Don't get too scared—or overly confident, either. There's a good chance that, when you sit down with your financial advisor, he will give you new information that may reverse your preliminary conclusion as to your status. Or he will be able to correctly interpret some data that you had misunderstood. So, instead of being *way* behind the eight-ball, you may be only *slightly* behind schedule to retire.

So reserve judgment. Again, it's like our medical analogy: you might feel a lump in your leg and worry about a blood clot—or cancer—so much that you can't sleep, or eat, before you meet with your doctor in two days. And then when he examines it, he is happy to inform you it's only an infected mosquito bite. Whew!

If you found, according to the interactive planner, that you do not have nearly enough money to last as long as your life expectancy, there is still hope. You may have to get creative, but hey—that can be fun. You'll want to focus on Chapter Six, "Playing Catch-Up: What to Do When It's 4th Down & 10." You'll need to reinvent your retirement.

On the other hand, if you found that you have much more money than you expected, money to last well beyond your life expectancy, preliminary congratulations are in order. Your biggest need at this point is to confer with your financial advisor to see if your calculations are correct. Keep in mind that the most influential variables that drive the interactive retirement planner are:

❖ Life expectancy
❖ Retirement age

❖ Retirement spending
❖ Accumulated investment assets
❖ Inflation rate
❖ Rate of return on investments
❖ Tax bracket

It's only through the use of a computer that you are able to experiment with 'what if' scenarios that are based on changes to one or more of the above variables. So you can experiment a little and see what effect the various factors listed above have on your retirement picture.

If you seem to be ahead of schedule, you may want to shape your plan to assure that your assets are protected; see Chapter Five, "Risk & Reward: How to Sleep Well at Night."

If you found that you have enough money to last to within five years of your life expectancy at least, you may be on schedule (or close to it). You will want to enhance this amount and optimize your plan. It's always better to have too much money than too little.

Now it's time to look at ways to squeeze more blood out of the proverbial turnip. Read on.

For example, you may determine, by using the retirement planning calculator, that your money is going to last until you're 80 years old. If you're comfortable with that, fine. But you might feel better— since people are living longer and staying healthier for longer—if your money were to last until age 90. In consultation, your financial advisor may be able to show you ways to make your money stretch if, say, you're willing to take a higher risk and earn a 12% rate of return vs. the 9% you had previously used. Alternately, he may warn you that if you want to have maximum safety and put your money in bank CDs at 6% rate of return, your nest egg may only last until age 75. With his help, you'll be able to make an educated decision about the amount of investment risk that's right for you. Or you may stick with a 9% rate of return and decide to work a few years beyond your previous target retirement age in order to build up your assets, which will push your end-of-money date out even further. And, as Martha Stewart likes to say, "It's a good thing."

A note about statistics—specifically about rates of return. When considering the changing economy and the financial markets during the next 30 years, you've got to be careful. Some financial advisors go with the stock market's past performance, based on more than 70 years of history, of an average rate of return of just above 11%. However, prudent planning would suggest single-digit returns: 8% or 9%. That way, if there are any surprises, they'll most likely be pleasant ones. Of course, no one has a crystal ball, but we just like to set up the equation with the odds slightly in your favor.

Once you've decided what rate of return you can plan on, you're able to calculate a rough idea of what income you can expect from your nest egg. For the sake of illustration (and keep in mind, this is greatly simplified), let's assume you have $100,000 invested. If that amount earns 10% a year, that's $10,000, which is $833 a month.

You smile, sit back, and say, "I could make it on $833 a month. That's easy."

But it's not that simple. Remember, Uncle Sam wants to get his greedy hands on his share, even when you're retired. So, you've got to be able to take $833 to an after-tax number. Depending on how much you "earn" in retirement income (and therefore which bracket you're in), after taxes you may have only $600 a month to actually spend. Is $600 sufficient for your needs? Only you can decide that, but your financial advisor can give you the help you need to make that decision.

One of the biggest factors many individuals overlook, when forecasting how large their nest egg must be someday to allow them to live comfortably, is the effect of inflation. Inflation, simply put, is the trend that, over time, makes our money buy less goods and services tomorrow than it does today. For example, our grandparents spent $20,000-$30,000 to buy a house, whereas today that dollar amount is often merely a down payment for a house.

There are various ways to achieve the same after-tax income, and your financial professional can explain these to you. In our example two paragraphs above, if you say that $600/month is *not* acceptable and that you'll need $833 *after* taxes, your financial advisor can calculate either how much larger the nest egg would have to be, or what higher rate of return you'd need to achieve to hit your target spendable income figure.

The point is, there are many ways to reach your goal. Stay relaxed (i.e., not panicked—our brains don't work well in panic mode), get the best advice you can, and remain flexible as to what options you might consider.

As an example of flexibility, if your calculations are looking somewhat bleak, loosen up your parameters. Maybe you and your spouse always had bigger and better houses as you changed addresses. And maybe you're proud of the huge house you raised your three children in, but they're gone and it costs a ton to heat and air condition. You might want to consider selling that big ol' barn and buying a small condo. You could let your financial advisor put the difference (e.g., your house sold for $200,000; your condo cost only $110,000) to work during the last ten years before you retire.

Hey—that $90,000 can make a *huge* difference in the hands of a competent financial advisor over time. It could make a significant difference in one of many areas: your end-of-money date could be extended, or you could take fancy vacations in your golden years, vs. going camping in a tent. Or it could move up (i.e., make earlier) your retirement age; you could be hitting the golf course earlier than you had expected. There are all sorts of options; the key is being open to trying some. You may have to swallow your pride (e.g., share one car with your spouse in retirement), or just change the way you view certain things (as in the condo example). The goal is to retire adequately and comfortably, and if it takes being radical in small (or large) ways, so be it. Your ultimate victory in achieving the kind of retirement you want will far outweigh any sacrifices you may have to make to do it. Keep your goal in mind and, with the right help, you can do it.

The core idea is simple, but there are many variables that enter into the equation in real life. That's why you need a financial advisor to help you. For example, take inflation. When your kids are growing up, you're subject to one inflation rate. When they are out of college, you may be subject to a different inflation rate. During the first 10 years of retirement, you are subject to another inflation rate; when you're over 75 years old, you're subject to yet another. That's because you're buying different things during those periods of time. You buy growing kids new clothes and new shoes all the time; you pay for big weddings at a certain age; you pay for a house or houses during your working years; in retirement you may not have many housing costs besides taxes on your home. In early retirement you may have more travel expenses; as you get older, you may have fewer trips and probably more medical costs.

A sophisticated retirement spending plan would thus insert four or five different inflation rates into the calculations. In addition, it will insert three or four different spending rates, because your spending changes as you age. The state-of-the-art, sophisticated budget software that a financial advisor uses will compute the exact tax that's due on the gross income.

If you (or a less qualified financial advisor—beware, they are out there) use basic forecasting software that is not so sophisticated, it will simply estimate an average tax rate, say 30%. That lack of precision gives you a totally different picture than computing the right tax for every year of your retirement plan. You should not accept anything but the best forecasting advice.

The more sophisticated your retirement planning software (and overly simplistic ones are of little use), the more need you have for a professional to steer you through the right hoops. He will tell you which of those hoops are worth addressing, and which don't make sense to jump through. Simple personal budgeting software (like often comes preinstalled on new computers) doesn't have to face what happens after you retire, the way your financial advisor does. The company that makes these simplistic programs merely prints a disclaimer on the bottom of the print-out that says, 'This software reflects figures we think are reliable.' As a point of comparison, why does a popular tax-preparation software package cost $39.00 while a CPA uses software he paid $5,000 for? There's a big difference between the two. Don't settle for second-best.

Good financial advisors will make suggestions that no off-the-shelf software program ever could. For example, in the state of Ohio, if you and your spouse each made $40,000 per year, you can save a lot of money by filing as "married filing separately" instead of "married filing jointly." A financial advisor would point out to you that there's a 'marriage penalty' for filing jointly if you have about the same amount of income.

High quality planning software in the hands of experienced financial advisors may also take into account changes in tax law and, based on an individual's needs, suggest certain changes each year. Many top-selling financial planning software programs (the cheap, off-the-shelf kind) have often been way off the mark because they treated qualified dollars the same as non-qualified dollars! So, as a consumer, look for the very best professionals you can find, in order to be as correct as possible in the process.

So now you have gathered your data and briefly analyzed the results of a basic retirement plan. It's time to move up to the next level.

CHAPTER 3

A Winning Game Plan: Choosing Your Team

I f you get only one concept from this book, get this: *Don't plan your retirement alone—get professional advice.*

Why not go it alone? Well, it's as if you had massive chest pain one night and sat down the next day with a cardiologist who recommended immediate bypass surgery after looking at your tests. You gulp, glance at your spouse, and agree to the surgery, thankful that you hadn't suffered a fatal heart attack in the night. In fact, you're even feeling a bit proud of yourself that you didn't put off this visit to the expert you're sitting with. You had the pain and went right in. Good for you.

Your doctor takes a few minutes to give you

and your worried spouse a preview of the operation to come. "I've been doing this type of surgery for 25 years and over that period of time, I've seen a lot of changes," he says. "Mostly changes in the health insurance area. These days, insurers won't pay for hardly anything, and our losses are starting to really add up.

"So what I'm going to recommend is a new procedure, called autosurgical fabrication. I'm going to give your wife twelve books on how to do heart surgery, eight magazines on the same topic, and a few web sites our patients have found helpful."

You glance nervously at your equally-puzzled wife.

The doc continues, "So go on home, Mrs. Smith, read up on the procedure, and be ready to cut your husband's chest open at 6 a.m. this Friday. You're just gonna love the cost savings from doing it this way—they're phenomenal!"

You and your wife make a mad dash for the door. You're sure you've just met the craziest cardiologist in the world—and you both resolve that, cost savings or no cost savings, you do NOT want to do-it-yourselves when it comes to heart surgery!

Sure, you may save a few bucks by going it alone, in terms of investing for retirement; magazines, books, and web sites surely do cost less than hiring a financial advisor. But trust us, it's just as crazy a strategy as our doctor gave in the preceding analogy.

There must be at least 50 magazines out there on how to manage your money. Books abound, as do web sites, classes, and seminars on investing in the stock market via your personal computer. So why not just study up a little and plan your retirement yourself? Well, having kept pace with such media projects for decades, let us tell you, the vast majority of them are designed with one purpose in mind: to sell copies. Magazines, especially, give the false impression that you can manage a fine retirement lifestyle just by doing a little reading. It's in their best interest to do so. Here's why.

Think about it this way: If a magazine *really* had the absolute best answer for a financial plan, they would print it and trumpet it from the rooftops. Then the next month they would print it again. But that would get old pretty fast; it wouldn't sell copies month after month, which is their real goal. So magazines change their content every issue, spinning the same material in different ways. Variety is the spice of life, right? One month they say technology is the best sector of the market to invest in. Yet a few months later their headline reads, "Technology is Overvalued." Sensationalism is the guiding principle of media hype. Being helpful to readers is not.

It's the same thing with golf magazines. Every month they proclaim to have 'the secret to a great golf swing.' Yet if they really did have *the* secret, they'd go out of business. To give you the secret of a golf swing that hits the ball down the middle, each and every time, would make them tremendously popular...for a short time. But then they'd be obsolete.

We have a complete set of issues of a popular

investing magazine aimed at the general public from 1992-1995. Each February and August, this magazine recommends the "best" mutual funds to buy. Over a four-year period, they touted a total of 51 funds. However, only one fund recommendation was ever repeated on the list. Are we really supposed to believe that over a four-year span, 50 funds magically became the "best," then mysteriously slipped into oblivion with the also-rans?

People are misled and confused by the constant variety of conflicting advice. The media shapes the data, and spews forth a virtual tidal wave of advice, giving people information overload. Information overload causes confusion, fear, and eventually apathy. Instead of helping consumers, it actually cripples them—resulting in an inability to take action, because people fear they're going to do the wrong thing. This we call 'paralysis by analysis,' and it's a crippling disease.

If you want to do the investing yourself, good luck. And be careful. There are some tricky investment vehicles out there. For example, one mutual fund may call itself 'The Bond Fund,' and be classified by the financial press as a corporate bond fund, but in point of fact owns mostly government bonds. Government bonds may react quite differently than corporate bonds, so it's important to know what the fund really owns. When this bond fund's return is compared to the corporate bond index by major rating services, it may be misleading and cause the do-it-yourself investor major headaches. He thought he was comparing apples with apples, but he unknowingly was comparing apples with oranges. Bottom line is, without the experience and specialized knowledge of a financial professional on your side, you can easily go astray trying to do the investing yourself.

When you go to buy a vehicle, a Jeep Cherokee is a Jeep Cherokee wherever you go in the country. A McDonald's cheeseburger is a McDonald's cheeseburger wherever you go in the world. But if you go to buy a 'balanced mutual fund' or a 'high-yield corporate bond fund,' while there are lots of funds that bill themselves that way, they may be giving you a chicken sandwich instead of the cheeseburger you ordered.

Today, there is a big push for truth-in-labeling laws, but this trend hasn't yet reached the mutual fund industry. You know you've got 2% milk because the FDA holds the milk companies accountable, with strict labeling guidelines. But not so in the investment world. The names may still declare that they are 'balanced' funds or 'growth' funds or 'growth and income' funds, but you need a professional to look inside the funds and categorize them in an accurate way—and especially in a way that makes sense for your retirement needs. This is just one of numerous benefits you receive from partnering with a financial planner.

Do the Right Thing; It's *Your* Retirement

What makes money management succeed is *teamwork*—a good partnership with a trusted advisor.

Take the story of Ted, a man who has survived cancer. His wife, Molly, is a lovely lady who enjoys volunteering with the Girl Scouts. Ted tells about their experience in deciding to put teamwork to work for them in retirement planning. He had worked in accounting for decades, so he was very familiar with handling money, yet still saw the need to team up with specialists in the retirement field.

Ted explains, "I retired early, at the age of 53; Molly was 50. We are presently 63 and 60 years young, as Paul Harvey likes to say. At age 53, I basically had no clue whether I could afford to retire or not. The only reason I thought of retirement at that age was, my employer, a large corporation, was being acquired. I knew enough about mergers and acquisitions to know that I might be offered an early retirement package, as the new management reshuffled the cards of their personnel under the merged companies. I was Vice-President for Accounting at the time, having worked in that industry for 30-plus years.

"Sure enough, I was offered an early-out opportunity, with a lump-sum severance package, and I have to say that it was very attractive. Ironically, events played out very well for me in what I chose to do. My boss, who was younger than I, told me that I didn't *have* to retire; he valued my experience and expertise, and said that I would have a job as long as he was there. Well, through a series of events, I chose to retire early, and do you know what happened just one year later? My former boss was let go! So I was glad I decided to 'take the money and run.'

"But as I say, at that decision-making time 10 years ago, I really didn't have a handle on whether Molly and I had acquired sufficient funds to retire, or if I had some more work to do. I went to the trust department at our bank, which was large and well-respected in our community, and talked with some of the trust officers.

"They certainly knew their stuff, in terms of how to use trusts in estate planning, but I found that they were single-minded specialists in that area only. I was struck with the persistent realization that I needed broader areas of advice, and that I had to keep looking. I needed legal advice; I needed tax advice; I needed insurance advice, and so on.

"One of my trust department contacts told me of an upcoming seminar on retirement planning options, and Molly and I attended. After the series of seminars, we were invited to sit down with a financial advisor for an evaluation of our particular financial situation, and so we went to that.

"Looking back, I am amazed at the amount of time the financial advisor spent with us, even though we were not yet signed up as clients. He began working up a retirement plan for us long before we had signed on the dotted line! I was trying to keep my options open by looking around at other sources for help, but by the end of that portion of the process, both Molly and I were so pleased that we eagerly signed up.

"Our financial advisor took the time to explain all these things in terms that we could understand.

Sure, I had worked with numbers for many years, but Molly had not. And, truth be told, I too needed to learn a lot about the investing world. (Molly later would joke with our advisor about how he never blinked when she kept asking the same questions over and over again, but patiently explained the answers until she got it!) Sure, I had a background in accounting services, but I too was a specialist. Focusing on how to pay for your retirement is different than everyday accounting concerns. And our financial advisor really showed his expertise in a variety of areas—taxes, insurance, and asset allocation. In short, I realized that I had found the one-stop advice source that I yearned for, after having talked with the trust department folks at the bank.

"Up until that point in my life, I had made a pretty decent income, so I didn't think much about what I would retire on. But then, in my early 50s, my employer's acquisition situation was dumped in my lap, so I was glad to find an expert who could help Molly and me make the decisions that were called for. We really hadn't spent much time thinking about retirement, let alone planning for it. We had probably spent a grand total of 10 hours on it.

"Our financial advisor showed us that investing was more of a science than we had previously considered it to be—we thought of it more as a sport or hobby than anything else. You know, my golfing pals would say they knew a key fact or two about this stock or that, and we dabbled in those some, buying and selling in an erratic fashion. But our approach wasn't comprehensive, and it sure wasn't backed up with solid research like we now benefit from. We went from a hit-or-miss approach to one of investing on a solid foundation. That sure feels good.

"We hadn't thought of the possibility of *growing* our retirement savings after we quit work. We had just a simple save-and-spend mentality. Our advisor showed us how to let our savings earn more money while we slept—a nifty concept indeed.

"Molly and I are fairly conservative people, and so we wanted to know how risky—or safe—the various options were. Our advisor got a feel for what our risk tolerance was, and gave us the advice we needed to take risks with a small portion of our overall nest egg, while playing it safe with the majority of it. For example, before we met our advisor, I would have never invested in overseas opportunities, thinking that there was too much risk and that the U.S. market was the only one worth committing to. But he showed us some proven foreign mutual funds that were worth a try, and they have paid off handsomely for us.

"Twenty years ago I was diagnosed with prostate cancer. I had surgery and radiation therapy, and, thank God, I have been cancer-free for two decades. Let me tell you, when you get a deadly illness, it changes your viewpoint about a lot of things. Your planning horizon goes from normal to very short-term: like how to stay alive until tomorrow. And as you come out of the danger zone, it lengthens out a bit, like staying alive 'til your six-month checkup, and so on. Gradually you get back to a measure of your pre-cancer viewpoint, where you can think ahead some. But for me, I guess I needed that corporate merger—and deciding to hook up with our financial advisor—to get my eyes on the rest of my life, to think ahead.

"Molly often reflects on the 'change in gears' we had to do when we went from our earning years to our retirement years. She rightly says that you go from focusing on *earning* money (and saving what you can) to how to wisely *spend* it. It sounds simplistic now that I say it, but really, that's the gist of it.

"When we first retired, even though we had plenty of cash and our advisor was telling us to relax, that things looked good, we couldn't bring ourselves to really spend our money. It was scary, knowing that each month I wasn't bringing home a paycheck. But the more we looked at the facts our advisor provided, the more we learned that it was okay to spend. We gradually got our emotions under control and can now relax and enjoy our golden years.

"The central emotion we get from working with our financial professional is trust. He comes across as a very honest person, a caring person, an open person. During our first few meetings, we knew we could feel comfortable with our advisor.

"One of the fun things in our relationship with our advisor is, we get invited to meetings where big shots in the financial world, like mutual fund managers (the guys who make the buy-and-sell calls each day) would tell us the latest news about our investments. These guys know our advisor personally; we could never dream of making these connections. So we get the feeling we're on the inside track, and we are, in a very real way.

"Today we know that if we have a question about anything impacting our financial health, we can pick up the phone and ask our advisor. He returns our calls promptly, and if he's out of town, one of his colleagues will step in and discuss whatever it is we need. Even though we know our advisor must have lots of clients, you could never tell from the way he treats us. When we speak with him by phone or in person, he's totally dialed in to us and our concerns.

"I have friends who are retired and who manage all their own investments. They proudly brag that they are 'saving all those commissions and other fees.' Yet the more I talk with them about how much time and energy they give to their finances—and how much worrying they do—the more I'm glad that I have a professional running our program. My philosophy is, let him stay up at night worrying about market conditions—I don't want to!

"And do you know what my friends are realizing, as time goes by? That the more they learn about the investment world and its fast-changing realities, they more they realize how much they *don't* know. And that keeps *them* up at night! If they own, say, $50,000 in Microsoft stock, they don't know if they should sell or hold their stock when the Justice Department's antitrust lawsuit ratchets up a notch or two on the evening news. I can't tell you how glad I am that I don't have to live aboard that roller-coaster!

"Our advisor has educated Molly and me very well on the investment world. I can confidently say that I know *the basics* of investing. But I don't know too much; if I knew all there was to know, I wouldn't sleep so well at night, and I wouldn't enjoy myself on the golf course, either. My bottom line on technical financial knowledge is, I know enough to sign up a pro to work for me. Really, that's all I need to know!

"I like that our advisor's approach is based on a *planning* process. It's a plan that we set up beforehand, one that we can then adjust as the market changes, or as our needs change. Like if my health takes a dive, God forbid, we can adjust the plan. Or if the market takes on a totally new posture—such as, if interest rates should double—we can adjust the plan. He showed us how the plan changes on purpose, too, as our ages climb and our needs may change, like if one or both of us needed long-term care.

"In the meantime, though, we can live life as we've dreamed: I play lots of golf and Molly gets to plan our travel and pursue her interests. We have time for enjoying our three sons and their families; to watch our five grandkids grow up; we have the financial ability to go on fancy vacations if we want to. Thanks to a lifetime of hard work and our advisor's help during these last 10 years, life truly couldn't be better."

The Team

While a partnership with your financial advisor is crucial to your successful retirement, there are other partnerships you also need to form. These partnerships constitute your team.

Yes, teamwork is the key. But how, exactly, do you put together the right team to win this game? Is it as simple as calling any financial advisor you find in the phone book? Not quite; having a qualified financial advisor is important—very important—but it's not the whole picture.

You need to create a retirement *team*—a group of talented people to assist you, the owner, in getting a touchdown: the kind of retirement you want. You need to gather certain qualified professionals, at a certain point in time, to kick off your game plan. Only a team-planning approach will ensure that what you see is what you're going to get. Your team of experts can interact with your wants, needs, and desires; they can advise you from different viewpoints and different areas of expertise. This is much more beneficial than choosing one financial advisor, who may claim (or imply) that he knows it all. Hey—there's strength in numbers, and with as complex a task as successful retirement is, you need all the help you can get.

To make up your winning team, you will need the following:

❖ a financial advisor
❖ an attorney who specializes in estate planning
❖ a tax advisor (CPA or equivalent)
❖ a banker
❖ an independent insurance agent

You Are the Most Important Player

Moving from the sports arena to a business model (as is often done—Lou Holtz probably makes more money speaking to business groups than from actually coaching college football), you are the CEO (Chief Executive Officer) of your retirement team. When you retire, you will leave one job behind—your profession, or the last job you had—and begin another: that of successful retired person. Successful in any way you define success: being a winner with family, recreation, volunteerism; you name it—that's the beauty of your golden years.

Now, every good businessman knows that a CEO cannot get into every nitty-gritty little thing that goes on in his company; that's what he has managers and employees for. There's not enough time in the day for that, and it's a poor use of his talent, which should be visionary and leadership-related. The CEO of General Motors doesn't know exactly how an engine is built inside the factory or what size wrench the workers use to tighten the bolts on a brake assembly. And that's as it should be.

In your retirement, you as CEO need to have an overview of the objectives as your primary focus, while you leave the smaller details to your experts. For example, you would know that you must get an 8% average return and remain diversified for safety. You don't need to know why you have 31% in large-cap value funds and 36% in small-cap growth funds this year. It's the engineer, the guy with the scientific calculator, who needs to know that. Of course, the CEO expects and requires reports from his teammates in order to monitor their direction and progress toward the goal. So it's not blind leadership on your part.

Acting as CEO, you soon realize that each of the professionals on your team comes from a slightly different bent. To each, a different aspect of your retirement will be deemed more important. Your key players may not always agree on the best strategy to protect and enhance your retirement fund—and that's as it should be. It's like when you get sick, if you consult a surgeon, the answer to all your problems is probably going to be surgery. If you consult a chiropractor, the answer is probably going to be adjusting your back. An acupuncturist wants to solve your problems with pins and needles; a psychologist will go to the pain you've experienced earlier in life. Everybody has a bent.

None of the viewpoints of your team members is inferior; they have differing opinions because they're specialists. But someone needs to be in charge. You are that person; it's you who ultimately makes the call, based on the expert advice you get, and based on your overall judgment as to what you want to achieve.

Every CEO has a right-hand man; he's often called the EVP (Executive Vice-President). Out of the list of professionals we've outlined here, your financial advisor is the one to make the EVP. With all due respect to CPAs, you don't want a CPA as second-in-command; nor do you want your attorney—legal expertise is too specialized. A well-rounded, experienced financial advisor has some background in all the areas that the other pros cover in depth, so he can help you interpret their input.

With a football team, the center is usually not too good at passing, the fullback isn't a great field-goal kicker, and the kicker doesn't catch passes too well. But the quarterback (i.e., the EVP) understands the role and function of all these activities, and he's the one the coach puts in charge of on-field, split-second decisions. His talents are best used for quarterbacking, not stopping the linebacker from blitzing, especially when the linebacker weighs 300 pounds! Likewise, the financial advisor is the best player to guide and direct the team members—under your direction, of course.

Choosing Your Financial Advisor

Financial advisors are the family practitioners of the financial world, but unlike doctors, they don't need to be certified. Certification is one indicator of their minimum knowledge base; this is helpful to you before you get to know them in the trenches. Like all professions, there are great planners who are not certified and lousy ones that may be certified. Certainly, there are many types of certification out there, but in our opinion, the best is the CFP (Certified Financial Planner). To attain this ranking, a financial advisor must pass six segments of exams, incorporating the major elements of the knowledge base of an attorney, tax adviser, banker, and life insurance agent. In their studies, they cover:

- ❖ The general financial planning process
- ❖ Estate planning
- ❖ Employee retirement plans
- ❖ Tax planning
- ❖ Investment planning
- ❖ Insurance planning

Your financial advisor's knowledge base will be broader in scope than that of any of the other professionals. Working under the Financial Planning Association's Code of Ethics, he practices seven principles:

- ❖ integrity
- ❖ objectivity
- ❖ competence
- ❖ fairness
- ❖ confidentiality
- ❖ professionalism
- ❖ diligence

He will get the rest of your team coordinated and keep them on track. He will be in charge of the scoring drive down the financial playing field.

Identify an Expert

One problem you may encounter when choosing your quarterback is that just about everybody claims to be a financial planner. Twenty-five years ago, 95% of financial planners were insurance agents in disguise. Today we joke that the figure is much improved—it's only 90%! The more things change, the more they stay the same. There are so few government regulations for those who are entering this business that you could go out tomorrow and say you're a financial planner, based on the fact that you wrote a high school research paper about it or that your brother is a CPA. Honestly, just about *anyone* can hang out a shingle and claim to offer financial planning services.

So beware.

You can't gauge a financial advisor's qualifications by his method of compensation. Some are compensated by commissions derived from buying or selling securities; others, by charging a yearly fee based on a percentage of the assets they manage for the client; others are compensated on an hourly basis. None of these methods is inherently better or worse; all are perfectly legitimate. Some fee-based planners may make the point that they are more ethical than commission-based planners. But nearly all fee-based planners used to be commission-based; that's how our industry billed its services almost exclusively, a few years ago. Method of compensation is neutral in the financial planning arena; it just depends on what fits the client's needs or desires. Many clients opt for paying a commission up front, and then yearly fees for services after that. What's most important is to understand the payment philosophy of the planner you are working with, and to feel comfortable with that arrangement.

A tip when looking for a financial advisor: A banker may not be the best choice. More often than not, banks have a high turnover rate, resulting in a lack of continuity with the people you work with. In addition, those people may be less experienced.

A Certified Public Accountant may not be the best choice, either. The simple reason? When you need his help, it had better not be between January and May, when the CPA is swamped with tax returns. Also, a CPA's retirement advice will be slanted toward lowering your taxes, which can be good, but there are more important variables that enter into retirement planning than simply how to minimize the tax man's bite.

Questions Are Key

The most important advice a financial advisor can give may have nothing to do with investing your assets. Rather, he helps you in your *thinking process*. When looking for your financial advisor, consider hiring the one who asks more questions than you do. That's right. The best financial advisor is the one who will not only answer all your questions, but also will ask questions you haven't even thought of. Asking the right questions is the key to a sound retirement planning process.

The best financial planner will expose your

blind spots. For example, let's say you were divorced 10 years ago. A good financial advisor will ask, "Do you know who the beneficiary is on your 401(k) plan?" You may have remarried and now have two children with your current spouse, but if you haven't changed the beneficiary on your 401(k), and you die, your ex-spouse will get every penny of it. These things are often overlooked, but not by a competent financial advisor.

Or, let's say you are 50 years old and you have $500,000 in a certificate of deposit (CD) at 6% interest. You're earning $30,000 a year on that CD, and you decide to retire now and live off the interest. A good financial advisor will ask, "Well, have you thought about inflation?" Five years from now that $30,000 isn't going to buy the same amount of goods it buys today. To illustrate, go ask your grandfather if he paid more for his *last new car* or his *first house*.

Some of the things a good financial planner will help you with won't show up in your first few meetings. A good financial advisor will not just offer investment recommendations. His real worth can also be in telling you what not to do.

Let's say you come across a hot stock tip. You see an opportunity to double your money. Your financial advisor points out risks you didn't see. You choose not to invest your life savings and, a year later, the company goes bust. If you hadn't listened, you would have lost a significant chunk of your net worth, and would have endangered your retirement. That advice didn't generate a return on your assets but it did preserve your capital, an equally important consideration.

Alternately, you get the urge to buy a new $350,000 home 10 years before retirement. Your financial advisor knows that if you stay in your current $150,000 home, you can easily afford to retire on schedule. But if you give in to that urge for the bigger house, you'll be taking a step backwards and could be jeopardizing your retirement.

Here's another consideration: Historically, women have longer life expectancies than men. This means wives may outlive their husbands. Wouldn't it be nice to have a financial advisor in place for continuity and comfort before the unexpected happens? Moral of the story? A good financial advisor proves his value to you in many ways.

Choosing Your Attorney

In picking an attorney for your retirement team, consider your personal situation. Unless your estate is quite large and complicated, you may not need the biggest law firm in your town. Not to knock the big firms downtown, but our point is, those firms are set up to primarily serve corporations, and there's a lot of overhead and cost involved. The biggest is not always the best, anyway. It's important to find an attorney who fits your specific needs.

It is equally important that you feel comfortable with your lawyer. If you've been with a certain attorney for a long time and feel comfortable with him, but he doesn't happen to be an *estate* specialist, it is essential to ask him to refer you to a capable estate attorney. Estate planning is so specialized that you want somebody who does it exclusively, because the laws change constantly.

The bottom line? Your financial advisor can help you find an attorney best suited to your needs.

Choosing Your CPA

When you were working, your company with-held taxes from your income and you got a W-2 form at tax time; sometimes you had overpaid taxes and you got a refund; other times you had underpaid and you owed the IRS money.

In retirement, nobody's going to be taking taxes out of your income. You may need to make quarterly estimated tax payments, so you'll need the help of a certified public accountant. The CPA you choose will need to know what kind of lifestyle you are planning in retirement, in order to make a wise estimate of what your taxes will be, down the line.

Just like you did for an attorney, find a CPA who suits your needs. Again, he needn't be in one of the large firms, if you have a simple tax return. But if you have a complicated tax situation, and your finan-cial advisor thinks your situation merits it, you may find it helpful to deal with a large firm that has resources to handle your needs.

Choosing Your Insurance Agent

You should seek an independent agent rather

than one who works for one insurer, because if he's a captive agent, he may experience pressure from his employer to sell only his company's products. With an independent agent, your choices are greatly expanded.

When selecting your agent, consider your auto, home, and life insurance needs in retirement. Your financial advisor can guide you in this confusing arena.

Choosing a Banker

Whether or not you'll want to include a banker on your team depends on the size of your assets. Private bankers may be good for people who have more than a million dollars, or who travel a lot overseas and may need a banker's help in a pinch. Big banks offer global services that frequent travelers may need. If you have assets held in trust at a bank, it will probably be important to have the banker involved with your financial planning. A lot of people inherit trusts that stipulate the trust has to stay at a certain bank. It is important to tie your trust into your plan.

Everything should work as a whole. If the bank has a tilt toward buying utility stocks, you want your financial advisor to know about this. A banker may look only at what the bank is managing for you, not at your other assets.

At a minimum, you want all the players on your retirement planning team to know about each other; and if possible, to know each other personally, to be on friendly professional terms with each other. They may never all actually meet together in the same room with you, but they may occasionally call each other to discuss some aspect of their advice to you. The main thing is that you, as CEO, want everyone clued in on what's happening. And you want your second-in-command, your financial advisor, to be comfortable with the team, too. You can use his recommendations in assembling your team, or you can choose your own players with his blessing, as long as they are qualified in the ways we discuss here.

Start Now

People think they don't need to form a retirement planning team *before* they retire. They say, "Oh, I'll get a financial advisor when I retire. I'll wait until I need one."

Let's think about that. Playing catch-up is often costly. It's not too early at all to begin putting the players together about four to five years before you expect to retire. Why not start building a relationship with those people *now,* so you'll understand the philosophy they're working with before you give them such a huge role in your economic future? That will give you the best chance for success.

CHAPTER 4

Stocks, Bonds & Mutual Funds: A Primer

Before we go much further, it's important to make sure you understand some of the basics of investing. It's been our goal from the start to minimize the amount of 'investing techno-talk' we use here, and keep the discussion on an understandable level for the average consumer. But while that's a noble goal, when you get right down to it, the world of investments actually *is* very technical—so we must do some translating.

Therefore in this chapter we'd like to explain the basic building blocks of investment vehicles: stocks, bonds, and mutual funds. Of course, more vehicles exist out there—some very exotic ones, if you look hard enough—but in the final analysis, these three types are the most useful to the vast majority of investors. Stocks, bonds, and mutual funds are, in effect, the three most important pieces on the chess board of the investing game. Let's briefly look at how they might help you plan and execute a successful retirement strategy.

Stocks

Stocks are *intangible assets* (as opposed to tangible assets, like real estate, gold, or works of art) that represent *ownership* in a company. They are, quite literally, pieces of paper—certificates—that give you certain very important rights of ownership. When you buy one or more of these certificates, called *shares*, you become a *shareholder* and you gain a say in how the company does business. Meetings are held regularly, and in these meetings you may vote on various important decisions the company is considering. If you attend in person, you vote in a normal manner, and if you choose not to attend, you may vote 'by proxy,' which is sort of like a mail-in election ballot. Naturally, the more shares you own, the larger your voice is in these meetings.

A stock is sometimes referred to as an *equity* by those in the financial services industry. Of course, equity represents ownership. Just like you have equity in your home, you have equity in companies issuing stock, if you own their stock. If you purchase shares of stock in a company, you are legally part-owner. You own a share of their buildings, their inventory, their computers—all their assets. True, it may be a very small part, but it's a part nonetheless.

Unlike owning a business directly, stock ownership has limited liability. For example, if you and your brother-in-law buy a bakery for $100,000, and someone gets sick eating your bread and sues you, you could potentially lose everything you have—much more than you had invested. That is, if you had each paid $50,000 to buy the business, and the lawsuit awards $1 million to the plaintiff from each of you, you'd probably have to sell your house and other assets to meet the judgment.

In contrast, stockholders are only exposed to *limited liability* for their company's actions. Let's say you own shares of a major airline that suffers crashes on half its planes in one day. If the families sue the airline for umpteen bizillion dollars and win, you don't have to lose everything you own; your loss is limited to the amount of your investment. If the airline should have to sell off its assets to meet the judgment (a highly unlikely scenario), your investment would become worthless—but that would be the extent of your losses.

Stockholders also have the right to inspect the corporation's books, as owners naturally do. But to prevent the chaos of thousands of shareholders demanding to be shown to the accounting department, an audited financial statement is periodically sent to shareholders, usually on an annual basis. Additionally, periodic statements are sent to shareholders, advising them of the company's performance and other pertinent information.

You may have heard the term "blue-chip stocks" on the evening news, or in conversations with your friends and associates. Companies that have been around a long time and that are considered fundamentally sound are called blue chips. They've weathered the test of time, such as General Electric, Johnson & Johnson, DuPont—companies that are currently respected by the market.

Curiously enough, the name "blue chip" comes from poker games, where chips are often used for betting. There are white chips, red chips, and other colored chips, each color representing a different denomination. Traditionally, the blue chips are the most valuable chips; hence this term is used to describe these types of stocks.

You can make money from stocks in two ways: dividends and growth. Some stocks pay dividends, which represent a share of the corporation's profits. These dividends are periodically declared by the board of directors and are expressed as a per-share dollar amount. For example, if you owned 100 shares of General Motors stock and the board declared a dividend of $1.50, you would receive a check for $150.

The main advantage of stocks is their growth potential. The value of your shares may increase as the company prospers over time. Historically, the stock market has outperformed every other investment category, including real estate. Since 1925, stocks have returned, on average, 11% per year. At that rate, you would have doubled your money approximately every seven years.

The downside of owning stocks is that they have a degree of risk to them, over, say, a CD you could buy at your bank, which is insured by the federal government. Owning stocks can be a little like riding a roller-coaster: Their value can go way up, but also way down. There are ways to control the negative impact of this rising and falling, a characteristic known as *volatility*. One tool to reduce volatility is diversifying through mutual funds, a technique we'll examine shortly.

Bonds

A bond is quite different from a stock. Whereas a stock represents ownership in the company, a bond is classified as a debt. A bond is a loan made by you, the investor, to a company or a government or a municipality.

Here's the heart of the concept of bonds: You, the investor, loan money to the company, and the company in return promises to repay you the principal plus interest over the time period specified. So, while a shareholder would have little or no recourse in seeking compensation for his loss if the company goes broke, the bondholder does. Just like you have to provide some security against defaulting on, say, your mortgage loan (usually pledging the lender your property, in the event that you fail to repay), so the bondholder has a claim on the company's property and other hard assets in case the company goes belly-up.

The difference between stocks and bonds is the difference between ownership and 'loanership.'

How safe are bonds, exactly? Well, there are some misconceptions out there, based on a lack of understanding about bonds. Prime among these misunderstandings is the notion that bonds are always 100% safe. In the case of a corporate bond, the value of the guarantee to repay is different for General Electric than for Joe's Corner Grocery. Clearly, you would be more comfortable loaning money to GE; its size, strength, and track record clearly trump Joe's.

As interest rates *rise,* bond values *fall*; conversely, as interest rates fall, bond values rise. If you don't hold your bond until maturity, interest rate changes may cause an unexpected gain or loss when you sell your bond. It's a lot more complicated than that in actuality, but those are the basic principles of bonds.

There are several types of bonds, among which are US Government bonds, non-US government bonds, corporate bonds, and municipal bonds. Each type of bond has its own unique investment characteristics.

Mutual Funds

For the majority of retirement-oriented investors, mutual funds are the best way to invest in stocks and bonds. Their popularity has grown since 1924, when the first mutual fund in the United States was created by Massachusetts Financial Services.

A mutual fund is a commingled pool of invest-ments in which you own an undivided share. It's as if you and your 25 neighbors each put money into an account and hired a professional to invest that money. Each of you would participate in earnings or losses in proportion to the size of your investment.

A mutual fund can purchase stocks, bonds, and other assets, as outlined in its prospectus (its legal handbook). The beauty of mutual funds is that they allow people with similar financial goals to pool their money into one professionally managed investment that has more power collectively than the sum of its parts. There is an efficiency and a synergy that bene-fits mutual fund investors that they couldn't achieve on their own.

The advantages of owning mutual funds are so great that *today the majority of US households partic-ipate in the stock market through mutual funds.* Stock buying and selling can be very tricky. Even with the tons of information available to you on the Internet, as an individual investor, you would find it impossible to gain the depth of knowledge on a company that pro-fessional fund managers have available to them on a regular basis. Professional fund managers adhere to an investment discipline which focuses equally on the buying and the selling process.

Mutual funds offer three central benefits:

❖ **A Millionaire's Diversification**. If you had a retirement nest egg of $5 million, it would be very easy to diversify your investment portfolio.

You could buy enough companies in enough industries to be properly diversified. But if you have less than $500,000 in your retirement account, it would be difficult to be properly diversified in individual stocks. When you are a shareholder in a mutual fund, you have the diversification of a millionaire. Diversification is the term for what your grandfather used to say: "Don't put all your eggs in one basket." If, for example, you put $20,000 of your nest egg into one mutual fund, your money would be spread out among several hundred companies.

❖ **Professional Investment Management**. You can bet that multi-billionaires have professional investment managers—some of the best in the world—handling their fortunes. But you, the little guy, would have a hard time attracting that kind of talent to manage your money. The pooling effect of mutual funds works in your favor here again. Taken together with that of fellow mutual fund shareholders, your money now has big-time clout collectively. Your dollars can now attract the highly talented (and expensive) professional fund managers who pick and choose the stocks, bonds, etc. for the group. And it's the expertise of these fund managers that can make the difference between making—or losing— money for you. Most ordinary investors couldn't get the attention of these managers—some of Wall Street's finest—because they don't have millions of dollars to invest.

The buy/sell discipline is where the rubber meets the road in investments: When is it time to buy something? And, harder than that: When is the right time to sell? Most of us can make the buy decision, given the time and the right resources to thoroughly explore an investment opportunity. But when is the right time to sell? When a stock doubles in share price after one year? You might think so, but what if a year later that same stock doubles again? If you sold off early, you would have missed some big-time gains.

Conversely, if that stock went down in value, should you sell then? Or, is it time to buy more?

Bottom line: Buying and selling individual stocks can be very tricky. Unless you have loads of time, resources, and aptitude to devote to your investments, individual stocks are not for you. Let the pros do all that legwork for you, and invest in mutual funds. You've got a life to live— and a retirement to enjoy!

❖ **Liquidity**. Another significant benefit of a mutual fund is liquidity, which means how readily available your money is to you while it's invested. Readily available investments are called *liquid*; those that are locked up/more difficult to cash out in a hurry are called *illiquid*. Are your funds locked up for a lengthy period of time? Or can you get at them in case of an emergency?

Real estate is an example of an illiquid investment. If you suddenly needed money, it could take months or even years to sell a piece of real estate, and even then the amount you receive may be less than you had expected. A money market account is a good example of a liquid investment; you can get your hands on the money immediately.

In the real world, people have unexpected family emergencies. Nobody plans on them, but difficult situations do occur: the death of a spouse, rapid declines in our health, etc. In retirement planning in particular, let's face it: We must make provisions for the unexpected, using a variety of tools, including liquidity.

The Value of a Trusted Advisor

There are many kinds of mutual funds available today. In fact, the number of mutual funds available at the time of this writing has reached some 14,000—more than the number of individual stocks! There are various types, or classes, of mutual funds, designed for various purposes.

With such a bewildering variety of options available to you, it becomes quite obvious why you need the expertise of a financial advisor. It is a confusing maze of alternatives out there. Your financial advisor can help you pick which funds to invest in, decide how much of your nest egg to put where, and coordinate the timing of all the operative factors as you work together to achieve your retirement goals.

CHAPTER 5

Risk & Reward: How to Sleep Well at Night

W hen you develop your retirement plan, you realize there are many variables that contribute to your plan's success. Some of these variables are easy to understand, like the age at which you retire, or what kind of spending habits you choose. A key component to your retirement plan is risk. How do you define risk? This variable is the most difficult to understand, partly because it carries an emotional component that can cloud our thinking at times.

Risk rears it ugly head in a variety of places. Most of us think of loss of principal as the only risk in the investment process. In reality, though, there are many more risks that are equally important. Let's take a look at some of them.

Interest Rate Risk

This is a little-known component of risk that must be considered in your retirement financial strategy. It has to do with how interest rates may fluctuate—up or down—over the years leading up to your retirement date, and during your retirement years.

Interest rate fluctuations can drastically affect the value of your retirement assets and may impact streams of income that you depend on during retirement.

Inflation Risk

This is the 'sleeper' factor that so many consumers either ignore or minimize—to their financial peril. Inflation is that economic force that diminishes your buying power over a period of time. It's why brand new automobiles in 1958 cost $2,155 and today cost upwards of $20,000. It's why a new home built in 1958 cost $12,000 and today would cost upwards of $200,000.

Inflation must be factored into your retirement plan, because in 30 years it will require more dollars than you could imagine today merely to buy food, heat your home in winter, and even play golf at your country club. A sound financial plan will incorporate inflation into your future and minimize its risk. If you don't plan for inflation, you're just fooling yourself.

Business Risk and Market Risk

These two concepts are distinct ideas, but people often confuse them, or lump them together in their minds. This is inaccurate and confusing, so let's set the record straight.

Market risk is the potential for an investor to experience losses owing to day-to-day fluctuations in the prices at which securities can be bought or sold.

Business risk, on the other hand, is sometimes related to the movement of the market price of a particular company's stock, but it is, at its core, a different concept. Business risk is based on the unfortunate truism that sometimes, bad things happen to good companies. For example, many years ago a sound, large chemical company, Union Carbide, suffered an ecological disaster outside its manufacturing plant in Bhopal, India. Hundreds of people died. Union Carbide made good on the damage to that community and fixed whatever technical problem caused the accident. But its stock took a pounding immediately, and it took a long time to recover.

Remember the Exxon Valdez oil spill in Alaska? Exxon, which is an excellent energy company, has been drilling and transporting oil and petroleum products safely for decades. But one day, the company's tanker ship strayed off-course, and the resulting oil spill destroyed untold numbers of pristine wildlife. Today the area is on its way to recovery, but in terms of public relations, it's a different story. Unfortunately, today many people remember Exxon principally related to that incident.

Or how about the bluest blue chip of them all, IBM? It has always been strong in making and selling mainframe computers. But then the company decided to get into personal computers, a new area for it, and its once-strong stock share price of around $140 eventually hit the low price of $40 two years later. Today it has made a rebound of sorts, but those two years were rough going indeed.

In all these cases, you have strong, well-managed companies that suffered a poorly-timed event, and their stock was hammered severely. You have to make allowances for this type of risk as you put together your retirement plan. You want the fewest surprises possible, while realizing that some surprises will always pop up. The goal is to be ready for them, as much as is humanly possible.

Emotional vs. Psychological Risk

As you consider the effects of risk upon your retirement, it's important to understand that there's a big difference between *emotional risk* and *psychological risk.*

The idea here is, people usually believe mentally that they can handle a lot more risk than they actually can, on an emotional level. In other words, you think that a precipitous drop in your portfolio won't bother you, but when the heat is on, you tend to panic.

For instance, you may believe in your mind

that you can handle a 20% decline on your $200,000 portfolio over one year, because you believe the market will eventually rebound. You know mentally that if you don't sell during that year, you won't lose anything when values improve. You're in it for the long haul, and therefore you can sit tight during that year, regardless of what you're hearing on the news.

But when you actually start experiencing the loss of $40,000 in one year, week after week, month after month, you agonize so much over losing that amount that you want to jump ship. You have stomachaches, you lose sleep, bags form under your eyes, your spouse worries day and night, and you're miserable. About nine months into the downturn, you give in to your fear and start selling off assets right and left, trying to cut your losses.

Unfortunately, that's when you can create *real* losses. A year later, the market does indeed rebound, and your assets aren't around to enjoy the bounce. You sold them at the lower prices, the previous year, losing serious money. Ouch.

Here again, this emotional vs. psychological risk quotient makes it important that a professional get involved in managing your assets. A good financial advisor operates according to a client's ability to handle emotional risk, not the ability to handle psychological risk. You cannot discern risk quotients for yourself; it takes another person who is outside your mind and your heart to do that. During each meeting, a good financial advisor will listen carefully to you. He won't just let investing happen; he'll look to discern your emotional vs. psychological risk quotient before he advises you on investing. He has two things which give him the upper hand in making his recommendations: [1] experience and [2] an emotional distance from your money. It's actually a big part of what a good financial advisor does.

It's like going to a doctor and saying you have constant headaches. He will test you—but what if nothing shows up on the tests? All the time you're together, he has been watching you and he notices that you squint a lot. He says you may need glasses. The problem is resolved because he used his professional judgment as part of the diagnosis process. A financial advisor will work with you in the same way as a good doctor.

As a rule of thumb, a person's emotional threshold is significantly less than his psychological threshold. And generally, that gap is bigger in men than in women. Women just seem to be better at understanding their true risk tolerance.

Of course, everybody can handle upside volatility (where market prices—and thereby values—go up quickly). But handling downside volatility is quite another thing. To tell where the rubber meets the road, your financial advisor will have multiple conversations with you about lots of things. He is looking for signals that will tell him about your ability to handle risks. That's important, because when people reach their emotional threshold, they may get angry—not only with themselves, but also with their financial advisor. So it is important that you have discerned your risk quotients correctly.

Now that all these risks have been brought to light, you may be thinking of putting your money under your mattress! But most of us need to earn a rate of return in excess of guaranteed bank CDs. To accomplish this, you must invest. So how can you try to level the playing field and reduce the various risks we have discussed?

Controlling Risk: Create an Asset Allocation Plan

In investments, risk is one measure of volatility—the rate at which values go up or down. In other words, how steep a roller coaster are you riding? The coaster made for three-year-olds to ride with their parents? Or the hair-raising monster that flips you upside-down three times and sends you stumbling off it onto terra firma?

There's a technical term called 'Beta' which Morningstar (a mutual fund rating service) defines as *a measure of a fund's sensitivity to market movements.* For our purposes here, we are going to somewhat oversimplify this complex concept. A Beta of 1.00 is defined as the actual volatility of the market, most often measured by the S&P 500. (The S&P 500 is a list of 500 stocks picked by the Standard and Poor company. This list is said to represent the U.S. stock market as a whole.)

Any variation away from the value of 1— whether above or below the S&P's actual performance—indicates a greater or lesser degree than the market's volatility. So if an investment is 20% *more* volatile than the S&P, it is said to have a Beta of 1.20. It means you're experiencing 20% more volatility than the market average, and you may therefore expect 20% more return. Conversely, you may experience a 20% greater loss in a decline. Remember, you want to be compensated for the risks you're taking.

In contrast, if an investment has a Beta of .80, that means it is 20% *less* volatile than the S&P 500. So if the S&P is up 15%, and you have a mutual fund earning the same rate of return, but which has a Beta of .80, that means you're earning the same return with a 20% less risk than the Index. That's good. You're accomplishing the same things with less risk.

Consider this chart; it shows various investments with their rates of return and their respective Beta values:

Investment	Return	Beta
A	15%	.80
B	13%	.80
C	20%	1.60

In the chart above, note that investment A and investment B have the same Beta, or amount of risk, yet A has a higher return. So A is a better deal. Note also that investment C is twice as risky as A (2 x .80 = 1.6). We might expect that if it is twice as risky, the return should be twice as good; but look at C's return: it's not 30%, but only 20%. Why take double the risk without double the return? So we can see by using

Beta and rate of return in a comparative analysis, A is a better investment, since it has the best blend of earnings and risk.

A side note seems appropriate here: Why have we entertained a technical discussion like this in a book that has thus far been purposefully non-technical? Reality. The reality is that good investing is a technically complicated process that most people should get help with. Yes, risk can be reduced, but it is not easy.

If you (or a non-sophisticated financial advisor) looked only at returns, and didn't factor the Beta coefficient in, you'd say C is a much better investment, since it earned more money. But that's too simplistic an approach. It's important that you understand the basics of Beta—and that you make sure your investment advisor is using it as a tool for balancing your risk in your portfolio.

In 1990, American economists Drs. Harry M. Markowitz, Merton H. Miller, and William F. Sharpe won the Nobel Prize for their Modern Portfolio Theory. What they were able to do is to mathematically compute risk, and the Beta coefficient was born.

Here is an analogy that helps beginning investors understand diversification. Picture two elevators side by side. One has two cables holding it; you notice that one cable is fraying. The next elevator has eight cables holding it, and again you note that one is fraying. Which elevator would you rather be in? Obviously the one with more cables—the one that *spreads out the risk of plummeting earthward* if that frayed cable breaks.

In investing for retirement, we want you to have multiple cables, too. If all the stocks you own go up, and all your assets are in one bucket, your return will be very good indeed. But that's a big 'if.' Predicting such a whiz-bang winning scenario is very difficult, if not impossible. We don't think it's worth the risk to put all your assets in one basket. Because nobody knows when things are going to go badly. Even Microsoft stock goes up—and down.

Sector Allocation

Some people make the mistake of thinking that owning 20 different stocks is always considered diversification. But if all 20 stocks are technology stocks, you still have all your eggs in the technology basket, or *sector.* Even though you would be well diversified within that sector, this does not translate into diversification for your portfolio. As technology goes, so goes your retirement, and that is just plain risky. A good financial advisor will help you make sure your allocation between sectors—such as transportation, technology, financials, industrial cyclicals, energy, consumer staples, and the like—makes sense for your risk tolerance and investment objectives.

Even owning four different mutual funds may not be considered diversification. Thanks to computers and sophisticated overlap programs, you may find that all four mutual funds actually own 90% of the same stocks. In such a case, you are no more diversified than if you had put all your assets into just one of the four funds. Pay careful attention to sector exposure when setting up and reviewing your portfolio. You should always use asset allocation with sectors in mind.

Don't Chase Returns

Another bit of advice we give clients is, "Don't chase investment returns." That is, don't look at history and decide that the future will automatically repeat itself, and jump into a stock that did well in the past for that reason alone. A common mistake people make—even some of our longtime clients—is to see that one of their investments lost 3% in the last two quarters, and another of their holdings went up 50%. They'll say to us, "Let's get rid of the 3% investment and put it into the 50% investment."

We tell them, "No, we're going to sell half of the 50% investment and put it into the one that lost 3%." It's a matter of perspective. We may see the 50% one as having hit its peak, and the time to get out may be near, but we don't panic, either, and so we sell only half. Conversely, we may see the minus 3% one as a buying opportunity (depending on our research; there was a good reason we got into it in the first place). Chasing returns is more often than not a dead-end street. As they say on the investment ads on TV and in magazines, "Past performance is no guarantee of future results." We believe in that.

Good financial planning is about guiding peo-

ple so that they're able to do the basics of any investing transaction: buy low and sell high. Let's say you
have five really good fund managers, each with his or
her own mutual fund, and four do well one year, but
the fifth does poorly. Do we automatically sell the
fifth fund?

No. We do our homework of course, but it is
more than likely that the fifth fund's area of investment had a bad year; it's not necessarily a reflection
on the fund manager. We may believe that, next year,
the fifth manager's area of investment concentration
will have a good year, and so we stay the course.
Certainly, you should constantly monitor your investments and make decisions based on history and fore-
casts, but this example is a typical one. Investing is by
no means a simplistic science.

Over- and Under-Weighting

One thing a financial advisor can do better
than most folks is to look at trends going on across the
economy and adjust your allocation based on that
forecast. This is called 'sector weighting.' If we think
international funds would be a good place to be, and if
we initially planned on putting 10% of your money
there, we might adjust that to 15%. Conversely, a
financial advisor might under-weight, going away
from certain sectors or funds that he/she knows might
present a negative risk situation in the coming months
or years. Learning to discern how to make these
adjustments is, of course, part of the art and science of

financial planning.

Be aware the financial planning process is still 15% - 20% art. Although the rest has become science, the art factor is still important to the person who needs the advice. You just can't go with some software you heard about; you have to add art as a secret ingredient. That's why you want informed experience at the helm of your ship. That's why you want the best humans you can find to advise you on retirement planning. Computers are nice, but only as tools in the hands of the best financial advisors available. That's why you need a financial advisor on your side. It's the best investment you could make toward having truly golden 'golden years.'

Age, Financial Math, and Being Compensated for Risk

Many financial gurus believe that risk in the market can be significantly reduced by time. True enough, if you just hang in there long enough, history has shown that your odds of having a positive return are fairly high. Unlike large corporate pension plans and charitable foundations that have an infinite time horizon, you have a finite horizon based upon your life expectancy. The closer you are to that time, the less time you have for your portfolio to recover from an investment loss. That is why financial advisors will often let a 32-year-old take on more risk than a 65-year-old retiree. Keep in mind that age is just one of many variables that should be considered in controlling risk. The size of your portfolio will also play an important role.

There is a distinction between 'life-altering money' and less critical amounts. This applies not only to amounts, but also to critical *ages* in relation to retirement age. The importance of working with an experienced financial advisor is all the more crucial when you think in these terms. If your money man is asleep at the wheel, you could be looking at some serious consequences for your lifestyle. So choose wisely.

Some folks come in with a rather cavalier attitude about losses; you know, 'Easy come, easy go.' Well, in retirement planning it's not quite that easy. For example, let's say your portfolio of $100,000 suffers a 15% loss one year (a loss of $15,000) due to market conditions. Let's say you're 62 and have just three years to go until your big moment. Well, the math isn't quite as simple as saying to yourself, *I've gotta earn an extra 15% to make up for that market downturn last year.*

The truth is, you have to earn *more* than 15% to get back to where you were originally. Do the math: Your nest egg declined from $100,000 to $85,000. The question arises: what rate of return do you need to attain, to get back to the original $100,000 level? Well, $85,000 would have to grow 18% to get back to $100,000. It's not 15%, which is what you lost. So recovering from losses is an uphill climb— down a slippery slope.

It can be done, of course, but the point is, you'll have to live with a slightly more aggressive investment to make it back. If you had used relatively safe investments that brought, say, 9% return to build up your $100K nest egg, that means quite an increase on the risk scale to go up to 18% return. It's about double the risk factor, in this example.

So now you can see why we are so risk conscious when it comes to investing our clients' assets. Gains are nice, but losses can be costly; more costly than merely making up the lost money.

Uphill climbs can be grueling, so we try to avoid them if we can.

A big part of our retirement planning concept is that for every risk you take, there should be some potential rewards. Think of it this way: If you're on the roof of a burning two-story house and you have to jump, you risk breaking your leg. But the risk is worth it because if you don't jump, you're surely going to die in the fire.

Now assuming that you jump and don't break your neck and die, you're relatively satisfied as you go to the hospital with a broken leg. You're almost happy because—hey, you're still breathing! You could say that the return on your investment of pain is 100%, in that you stay alive.

In contrast, if you're on top of a two-story house that is *not* on fire, and you want to get down as quickly as possible (maybe you're late to an appointment with your financial advisor), we're not sure jumping is worth the risk. Better to take a few minutes more and walk down the stairs. In that case, the risk of breaking your leg would not be worth the reward of saving a few minutes' time.

Brought into this discussion, if we could show you that you could go to a bank and get 7% return on a CD, and if we alternately offered you stocks at a 7% return, what have you gained by taking the additional risk of investing in stocks (where your principal isn't guaranteed, like the CD's is by the federal government)?

The answer is, you've taken a lot of additional risk and accomplished nothing. You gained no additional reward for your additional risk. The moral of this story is, if you're going into stocks, you'd better be able to earn substantially more than 7%. There ought to be a potential reward for taking on the additional risk over that of a bank CD.

Well, that's enough about risk. Now let's look at fine-tuning your plan.

CHAPTER 6

Playing Catch-Up:
What to Do When It's
4th Down & 10

I f you found, working through the material in this book, that you don't have enough money to retire, you're probably in shock.

You may have found that you are able to retire, but not nearly in the lifestyle you had wanted. Or you may have discovered that you will be able to live the lifestyle you want, but must work until you're 85 to finally achieve it! You may be feeling dismay, dread, sorrow, and even shame—but take heart. There are *many* ways to change your financial picture as it affects your retirement. Thankfully, there *are* ways of playing catch-up.

At least you're not alone. According to wire service reporter Bill Greenwood, a recent study shows that 56% of U.S. households say they aren't saving enough to retire comfortably. A shocking 59% of American families expect to suffer hardship in retirement. Only one in four U.S. households has sufficient funds for retirement.

If you and your financial advisor have concluded you have not saved enough money to retire, it means one of three things:

❖ You need to save more
❖ You need to spend less in retirement
❖ You need to work longer before retiring

You're Not Saving Enough

At some point in the process of assessing your present fiscal situation and projecting your retirement resources, your financial advisor may tell you, "You've been living on $4,000 per month. But based on your assets now and their projected growth, you will have to live on $3,000 per month in retirement." Then, together, you create a spending plan to keep your living expenses within $3,000 monthly.

You'll look at expenditures item by item. Food probably isn't going to change—unless you're presently spending a lot at restaurants. You may eliminate a car payment, or drive a Honda instead of a Lincoln; you may choose to create your own entertainment instead of attending concerts every week;

there are myriad options that you might choose.

Go through each category and try to see where you can save money to fit your new budget. Then you can readjust your lifestyle and move forward. Honestly, this process is not hard; the difficult part, that part that gnaws away at you at night when you can't sleep from worrying, is *not knowing* if there'll be enough for retirement. Trust us, it's better to live on less and be able to sleep well at night, than the opposite. Countless clients have experienced this peace of mind and they will all tell you that it's worth it.

Some people may be living on $120,000 a year now. However, a retirement analysis indicates their assets will only support $70,000 in retirement income per year. They'll usually say, "No problem."

In a case like that, it *is* a problem. You can't just go from $120,000 to $70,000 with the flick of a switch. When we share this, it surprises them a bit.

"Oh yes we can," they assert. "We'll just cut back some."

So we suggest some homework. A lab experiment, shall we say? While they're still working, they switch to that retirement budget for a period of time, to try it on, in a sense. A trial period of anywhere from one to three years is appropriate.

If they can make the changes and not go crazy (or get divorced!), fine; they're home free. But if they realize they don't like that lifestyle, they come back motivated to *do something about it*. They can work several years longer before they retire, or they can let their assets work harder for them; there are a variety of aggressive strategies to consider.

The point is, you have to decide *early* about your choice of retirement lifestyle; if you wait 'til the day you retire and then you don't like it, it's basically too late to do anything about it. Oh, sure, there are some things you can do at that point, but those options are going to be more painful than if you had taken the bull by the horns earlier.

If a couple says they've always wanted to play golf during retirement, they should start now. They should buy the golf clubs, take the lessons, and maybe join the country club, because they may not have that kind of cash in retirement. They get a trial run.

The Credit Card Two-Step

If you've got a credit card problem (i.e., if you carry balances instead of paying them off each month in full), it's essential that you figure out what that debt is costing you, and then create a plan to become debt-free.

You can't do that just in your mind; you've got to get it down in writing. Sit down with your spouse and your financial advisor and come up with a battle plan. It very likely will involve developing a budget and being tough on yourselves, so that you're not spending more than you are earning each month. It might involve cutting up your credit cards and going to an all-cash basis for your daily and monthly spending patterns. One nationally-syndicated radio talk-show host we know says that *all* credit card usage is problematic and recommends getting out the scissors as soon as possible. While we don't quite go that far, we agree that using credit cards when you cannot pay them off in full each month is like playing with fire. Eventually you will get burned.

Using an all-cash system has its advantages, though, in that you are forced to become quite concrete and tangible in terms of whether you should buy this or that thing. You make a collection of envelopes, one for each spending category, and cash your paycheck (instead of depositing it), dividing up each category's allocation of cash according to your budget. When it comes to the buying decision, it's simple: if it's in the budget and there's cash in the envelope for it, you may consider buying it. If not, not.

Try this little experiment: Lay a credit card out on your kitchen table, and right next to it, a crisp $100 dollar bill. Ask yourself, which of these two forms of money is more precious to you? That is, does it hurt more to give a merchant that hundred, or to slide your credit card across the cashier's table? The truth is, most of us have more of an emotional attachment to 'the green stuff,' and therefore we will think twice before plopping it down for a purchase, vs. simply signing a credit-card slip.

Another thought-provoking exercise for those with out-of-control credit-card temptations uses ice. Instead of the extreme solution of cutting up *all* your credit cards, you pay off and cancel all but one. The fact is, a credit card is necessary from time to time in modern life; for example, most rental car agencies won't rent you a car even with cash; they absolutely require a credit card. Here's the trick: You put your last credit card in a drinking glass and fill it with water. You place it in your freezer. When you're in a store and the temptation grips you to buy an item that's not in your budget, your credit card is not available. If you go home and think about it, perhaps discuss it with your spouse, etc., and then still feel the purchase is warranted, you simply defrost the credit card. That period of waiting for the ice to melt has prevented more than one impulse buy, and saved untold mountains of cash. Food for thought.

One technique that has helped a lot of clients is to make a chart that has the dates and the amounts of debt-reduction written in a calendar-style arrangement. For example, at the end of June you write, "Pay $300 extra on Platinum Visa—$1,700 to go." Then at the end of July you write, "Pay $300 extra on Platinum Visa—$1,400 to go." This way you can keep track of what you're working on, and you can't ignore it ("Out of sight, out of mind"—so hang it over your dresser or on your bathroom mirror). Plus, you are encouraged as you make progress, however slowly, toward retiring that crushing debt that is trying to drag you under.

We can practically guarantee that once you've made this chart, you will pay off debt faster than the dates you planned on. That's because when you get the numbers down in black and white, you immediately get competitive. You've got a goal, a crusade, a campaign to win. Here's what will happen: When you get a $100 refund on, say, a bill you mistakenly paid twice, your first impulse might be to go out with your spouse to a movie after a high-ticket dinner. Then you'll remember the chart and think, *I could get ahead on my debt-reduction chart with that $100.* Suddenly, you know the movie and dinner are not worth it anymore. You choose instead to rent a video and cuddle with your honey on the sofa in front of the fire. You come out way ahead.

Our bottom line on overspending via credit cards is: Sit down with your financial advisor or some other bona fide credit counselor and hammer out a plan. There are so many Americans in credit trouble today that an entire industry has sprung up to help you in this area. The focus of this book doesn't allow for an in-depth discussion of credit-card disaster relief, only for how crucial it is to resolve this problem. Get help if you need it. In almost every city in America, you can find consumer credit counseling agencies in the phone book. Some may charge a small fee; others are free. Even if it does cost you a small amount for their help, it's worth every penny.

Reality therapy. It may sting a bit at first, but down the road you'll be glad you took it. Controlling your expenses is one of the most powerful ways to increase your retirement nest egg and make your goals attainable.

School and Housing Choices

In addition to credit card debt, another major reason people are unable to retire on time (or in the style they desire) is because they're trying to pay for their children's college educations using the money they actually will need to live on in retirement some-day. The brutal truth is that today, with college costs having skyrocketed, many parents simply cannot afford to pay for all of a child's college expenses. They may have to consider it a joint venture, where they split the costs with the student, who can either work their way through school, or take out student loans, or both. And you may have to choose the state university instead of Harvard or Yale, but hey—many state schools provide excellent educations, at a good value.

An additional reason people don't have enough money to retire is because they are trying to finance a house they can't really afford. Now, this is an emotional issue—the main reason people may cry to their financial advisor is because they've been told they have too much home for their income. They will have to move, or they'll never be able to retire (at least not according to a plan they would like). Here, you need to deal with the non-financial issues involved.

The truth is, your ego is tied to your home. If you move into a smaller place, friends and family are going to think you're going downhill, that you've failed in some way. The American Dream usually involves moving up, not down, in house size. You've got to find a way to deal with the expectations of oth-ers. Perhaps you need to learn to reframe and restruc-ture your thoughts and emotions around this issue. Perhaps you need to have a heart-to-heart talk with yourself (or your spouse) and address the core issue: *Do I really have to keep up with the Joneses?* Or the thought, *Is it wise to steer my ship by what my neighbors or coworkers think?* However you do it, just know it's more important to be able to retire in a manner that's pleasing to you (not the Joneses), and to live relatively stress-free, than it is to live in a huge house.

Be careful about blind optimism. You know, saying, "Oh, I believe somehow it will just work out." There's nothing wrong with optimism, but sometimes this can be a cover for the fear of not knowing what to do to achieve the retirement you want. That's why we've written this book. We believe very strongly that optimism is great, but that it must be based on sound financial planning and execution of a plan.

You must ask yourself, "How exactly *will* it work out?" You have to start thinking about these things *before* you retire. Maybe you could sell that $500,000 home you're living in, with its $300,000 mortgage, and buy a $100,000 condominium, putting the other $100,000 of equity to work for your retirement. An extra $100,000 can make a whale of a difference over time, in growing that retirement nest egg. For example, $100,000 invested at 10% for 20 years will grow to approximately $733,000.

We've developed a house affordability index that you can find on our web site. This is important, because when the bank figures how much you can afford for a house, they use your gross income to figure against; that is, your income before taxes are taken out. We feel that's too risky—net income (take-home pay, after taxes) is better, since that's what you actually have to spend each month. We figure 25% of your net income after taxes is your upper limit for a housing payment. Our figure is going to be much less money than the bank says you can afford.

We often tell people, "You can afford a $200,000 mortgage, tops."

They reply, "That's funny—the bank says we can have a $350,000 mortgage. They prequalified us for a loan just yesterday."

You know why the bank's figure is higher than ours? Because the bank sells money. Bottom line for them is, the more money they loan out, the more they make in interest. Bankers are bottom-line people, and no amount of nice smiles and comfortable lobbies can change that. Ultimately, they don't care if you are 'house-rich and cash-poor.' They don't care that you pull up to a beautiful house that you can't afford to furnish properly. They don't care if your budget is stretched so tightly that if the car needs a $1,200 transmission repair, you have to borrow money off your credit cards to fix it.

Can you afford the monthly mortgage payment? Yes. Can you afford the mortgage *and* college tuitions for your children *and* retirement in a comfortable fashion before age 89? No way. Especially when it comes to housing costs, you have to keep *your* interests clearly in mind, not the banker's interest. Let him go sell big home mortgages to other people; you, in contrast, are master of your own fate, and you are going to retire according to plan. Besides, it's easier to cut the lawn of a smaller house.

How Diane Did It

Diane was very single-minded when it came to her housing choices; indeed, when it came to *all* her expenses. At the time of this writing, Diane was 60 years old and retired in Florida. She tells about how she combined her lifelong habit of carefully watching her expenses with her decision in her 50s to take advantage of financial planning to produce a stellar retirement. She found that she didn't have to play catch-up when she was approaching retirement; her lifetime thriftiness put her in a strong position as she shifted gears to retirement.

"I worked for a bank for 37 years, and over that time I saw a lot of changes. In the last couple of decades, many of the employees I managed got downsized—a nice word for let go, due to reorganization, mergers, acquisitions, etc. Well, often when that happened, the worker was given a relatively large termination package that included severance pay, the proceeds from their 401(k) account, a lump-sum distribution from their pension, and the like. I can tell you that for many of my people, to get, say, $25,000 all in one blow was quite stressful. Not that they didn't want the money, but the pressure was on them: *What to do with all this cash?* If you're used to handling, say, a $300 paycheck every Friday, having a big pile of money land in your lap can be mighty confusing! I'm talking about bank clerks, check-processing staff, and support staff. These folks didn't have MBAs, let us say, so this type of occurrence usually left them a little confused and stressed-out. And keep in mind that at that particular moment, they're suffering from a double-whammy, since they've just been told they'll soon be unemployed.

"As their manager, I wanted to be able to point them in the right direction for the kind of financial advice they needed. Let me underscore the fact that I'm pretty picky when it comes to giving referrals. Not only is my personal reputation for helping my staff at stake, but also the bank's reputation is too, indirectly. So I do my homework when it comes to giving my staff referrals for financial help.

"I first met my financial advisor through one of my staff who got downsized. This man was not caught flat-footed, however, in terms of getting financial advice upon his departure. He had found his 'money guy' long before he got let go. He was always raving about his financial professional, and for a period of a couple of years he kept telling me that his financial planner was awesome, and all that.

"Well, the next thing you knew, I heard my bank was being merged with another. And, as often happens in offices where the scuttlebutt is 'merger,' I figured my job function might be eliminated. And I thought of that employee who had always raved about his financial professional. He had been telling me for a couple of years to not wait 'til retirement to find an advisor, but rather to find someone I could be comfortable with beforehand. So I thought, *I'll call his advisor and see if he can help me.*

"I first met with my advisor in 1992, when I was 52 years old. I sat down and said, 'It's rumored that my employer might merge with our competitor, and if I get downsized, I need you to tell me what I should do, financially.' That didn't faze him one bit; my situation was 'old hat' to him, even though it made me quite nervous. He started analyzing my financial situation, and, to make a long story short, I was stunned to hear him say at the end, 'Diane, if you get downsized tomorrow, you could retire early—and live quite well for the rest of your life.'

"I was stunned all right, but pleasantly stunned. I never thought of myself as having much in terms of money. I was raised in the South by a single mother and we didn't have much—we were middle class, but just barely! Mama taught me to be frugal and to save aggressively for a rainy day. For example, when I was 15, I got my first job. I earned $15 per week. Mama said I had to save $5 of that. Thirty-three percent is a pretty good start!

"Anyway, by the time I had reached 52, even though I was a single mother myself (I'd been divorced since 1966), my advisor informed me that I had quite a little nest egg saved up. I have never liked talking with anyone about my money (which is ironic, since I worked in a bank for all those years and talked easily with folks about *their* money). So I guess I just kind of avoided the idea of totaling up all my accounts, even to myself. I never thought of myself as being rich, or anything but middle class (and not even upper middle class, which I guess I could qualify for, now).

"So it really blew my mind when my financial advisor said I was in a position not to have to go find another job, if I lost mine. Well, it turned out that I *did* lose my job in the merger, as I had feared. But with my advisor's help, I didn't panic. I just kept telling myself that I was okay, that I didn't have to scramble financially. And who would believe that little ol' me, a woman who never got a bachelor's degree (well, I did go to two years of business school), is now, in her golden years, worth more than three-quarters of a million dollars?

"I still have trouble believing it's true. None of my friends would even guess I've got that much money! I don't live in a flashy way. I prefer to drive a Honda Accord, not a Lexus, even though I could go out and buy a new one tomorrow. I've got nice clothes, sure, but I don't wear a big mink coat to church when it snows, and I don't flash diamonds around on my fingers, either. I'm just not an extravagant person; I've never had money and it still hasn't really sunk in that I do now, either! I was just a hard worker for many years, and my mother taught me to be a good saver and to live within my means. I took modest vacations, or no vacations at all; I bought a smaller house than I could actually afford; things like that. I guess it just all added up over the years. And I said my prayers! The Good Lord has sure blessed me, and for that I'm thankful.

"Well, once I retired I moved to sunny Florida

to be near my daughter and her two kids. I loved Cleveland, but I'm glad to be done with snow! My son-in-law owns a restaurant in the Orlando area, and I enjoy seeing my grandkids grow up. I can take 'em to Disney World any time I want. My former employer has branch banks in Florida, so even in retirement I'm training clerks and other operations personnel part-time; instead of me being an employee, they just call it 'consulting' now.

"I've enjoyed working with my advisor because he's so comfortable to be around. He's very competent in his profession, so that puts me at ease. As I say, I've never enjoyed talking about my money with anyone, so I was nervous to begin with. But my advisor put me at ease; he was relaxed and confident, and that kind of rubbed off on me. I began to feel relaxed and confident, too, about my financial future. And that comfort level has benefited all the folks I've sent to him—from janitors to executives at the bank, my advisor has treated them all first-rate, which reflects nicely on me.

"And of course he gives me good advice. Like early on, I had a lot of stock from my employer, and he suggested I sell it and buy into a mutual fund that had a good track record. That tip was a godsend to me. Because not soon afterward, that stock took a nose dive—and it didn't take me with it! I could've kissed the guy! I knew right then that it was worth the money to hire a financial advisor.

"As a result of my financial good fortune, I'm now in a position to help out family members who may be stuck in special circumstances. For example, I have an auntie who lives in California who is old and sickly, and she borrowed on her house to pay for her expensive medicines. Well, she got behind in her payments and was in danger of losing her home. So I wanted to help her.

"I called my advisor and asked him how I could best help my aunt. He got hold of an attorney in California and researched how I could pay off my aunt's home loan, which was at an exorbitant interest rate. Then, instead of her having to pay me back, she could just sign a deed over to me that would transfer upon her death. My advisor said he didn't want the house to be in my name now, due to liability and other financial considerations. The good news was, my aunt could forget about making those nasty payments, could stay in her home, and just focus on quality of life in her remaining years.

"My advisor helped me most by organizing all my financial affairs. For example, I had some insurance I didn't really need; he canceled some policies for me and consolidated others. And I had money scattered around in all sorts of different accounts: some here, some there. He brought it all under one plan, and that helps me a lot with my peace of mind. He knows at what point I need to start gifting money to my grandkids; he knows how much I can earn by consulting in retirement without triggering tax consequences, etc. He's my one source for advice when it comes to money; I love this guy!"

Change Your Mindset

If you'd planned to retire at age 65 and you realize you can't afford to do that, then you've got to change your mindset entirely. Do the math: how much do you need to retire on? If your retirement savings are only going to generate $1,000 a month and you need $2,000 a month to live on, you may have to continue to work, somehow. You will have to find a job where you can make an extra $1,000 per month. Maybe you can find something you enjoy. If you like golf, work at a golf course—or manage one (they usually give you all the free golf you can play). Or if you like books and gifts, work at your church or synagogue bookstore, or your public library.

Jobs like these won't make you rich, but then again you don't need to survive off them, you just need that supplement to make up the shortfall. And at least you'll be doing something you love, which is more than many people can say about their 40+ years of working before retirement. Above all, don't consider yourself a failure because you had to keep working beyond the normal retirement age. View it as a proactive strategy, vs. a reactive obligation.

The nice thing about Americans is that once we know what our problems are, we mentally re-map a way to deal with them. That's a fine thing. We say to ourselves, *Now we've got our new plan.* It feels better. But it still takes focus and structure. You have to have a road map. And that road map has to be written out, every step of the way, for every year until retirement—and beyond.

The important thing is, you've got to follow the map. You have to do whatever is necessary to rework your retirement plan, or you're going to be living miserably on Social Security and/or imposing on your grown kids, neither of which is very appetizing to most retirees.

Seven Steps to Reinventing Your Retirement

If you don't have enough to retire on, and you want to correct course, there are seven steps to successfully doing that. Focus on one step at a time. Create a structure with a financial professional, and follow it religiously from now until your hoped-for retirement. It's never too late re-engineer your retirement. With comprehensive planning, personal discipline, and a little luck, you can make progress you had previously thought impossible.

1. Realize there is no magic pill. You can't turn $20,000 into $200,000 in three years, instantly solving all your problems. It's not going to happen. But if you focus and follow the map, moving forward with each step, you'll get there. You have to accept the reality that things may not be exactly as you'd hoped. You will have to readjust your plans. To do that will take some creative thinking. Changes will have to be made, but as you make them, you will discover alternatives you had not considered. It won't be nearly as painful as your fears predict.

2. Reassess your lifestyle. You may have to take the bitter pill and cut your spending. To cut your spending is a big step forward. Refer to the cash-flow and budget information you gathered earlier. Where is your money being overspent unnecessarily? Make a list of the offending areas. Then ask yourself the hard questions. What can we do without? What is the difference between living well and living luxuriously? Are we trying to keep up with the neighbors and/or adult family members, siblings, peers at work, et al.? There are many ways to simplify and economize; brain-storm ways of spending less. Realize that every dollar you save now will go toward funding your retirement dreams.

3. Reevaluate your career plan. Perhaps you could work longer than you expected—if your health allows it, why not? Your financial advisor will help you calculate how much more you could contribute to your nest egg's growth by working two years more, or five years more. You might start looking now for an alternative job—perhaps something that will involve you in a hobby-turned-money-making venture. It helps to work in an area you're naturally interested in. There is a best-selling book whose title conveys a key thought here: *Do What You Love, the Money Will Follow.* You might start up this venture as a side business now, and then, as it grows, you could take it up as a full-time job, or a post-retirement vocation. If you're unsure of what area you're gifted in, go to a career counselor and learn about your options in putting your skills and abilities to work. Lots of senior citizens are showing up there nowadays; some because they don't want to retire—they feel energetic enough to keep contributing their skills in the marketplace.

4. Set goals. Sit down with your spouse and determine target dates to achieve your plan, step by step. Things you might include are:

> ❖ Calling the realtor to put your house up for sale and starting to look for a less expensive home

> ❖ Putting that extra $200 per month into retirement savings, based on your new expense reduction strategy

> ❖ Helping your child apply for college scholarships

Post these dates where you see them daily. Project your savings into the future and write the projected plan down in black and white. Refer to it monthly or quarterly to see if you are on track.

5. Create a spending plan. Start with the hidden assets you identified in Chapter Two. Maybe it's time to sell that $50,000 Lincoln Navigator and get a $14,000 two-year-old Honda Civic. Check out an online auction site and think about possibly putting your antiques up for sale there. Make decisions about what things you will definitely not spend more money on; write those down. Seek out ways to save on the things you consider necessities (e.g., buying groceries in bulk at a warehouse club, vs. small quantities at the convenience store), and make a list of these. Create a colored graph to show where and how you will save and what your retirement income will look like as you do. The gist is that you need to figure out how much money you can spend a month, maximum, and then hold your feet to the fire. Someday, down the road, you'll be glad you did.

6. Get professional help. Make an appointment with a debt counselor if you have credit card problems. Make an appointment with a financial advisor to answer the questions you've been asking. They will be able to help you do what previously appeared impossible. There are lots of potential mistakes you could make in the process of setting up a retirement plan, but your financial advisor will help you avoid them. There are some great ideas in your financial advisor's head that can save you big money—in this book we've only scratched the surface. A professional will be able to discern whether you are over- or under-reacting to your situation. Any one of us can take a splinter out of our finger; you don't call a doctor for that. But when you can see the bone after cutting your finger, you've got to get professional help fast—or you can do permanent damage. For some of you in this retirement planning process, we're starting to expose bone. Take prompt and decisive action; don't wait for that mythical day when your problems will all have fixed themselves. It won't happen if you don't make it happen.

7. Optimize investments. People who are on schedule (or ahead of schedule) for retirement can afford to use conservative investment vehicles. But if you're behind the eight-ball, you need to optimize everything you have. That's why it's so important not to go it alone; you need all the advice and strategies you can get. You can't afford to let a rather meager nest egg sit around for a year while you think about what to do. There are many things you can do; for example, you can use online banking to get a competitive rate paid on your checking and money market accounts instead of using your traditional checking account (where no interest is paid) and a traditional savings account (where pitiful interest is paid, like less than 2%). Or maybe now you're paying your insurances monthly with a surcharge added each month. It may not seem like much, but these may amount to 15% of your costs. So by paying it annually, you get a guaranteed 15% return.

It's never too late to make adjustments to your lifestyle and spending patterns during your working years, to build a satisfactory retirement. Your financial advisor will work hard at optimizing your money with strategies like these—and a whole lot more. If you're willing to take a hard look at what he finds, and are open to taking creative steps to change things, your chances are really quite good.

CHAPTER 7

Perfecting the Plan

U p to this point we've 'covered the waterfront' on the basics of financial planning for retirement. We've looked at gathering your data, pulling together all the pertinent information that describes exactly where your financial situation stands now. We've looked at how to analyze that data and reach some conclusions about what you need to do to reach your financial goals for retirement. We've examined how to put together a team of experts to help you in your quest; we've looked at how to manage risk; we've unveiled the basics of stocks, bonds, and mutual funds.

Now that we've covered the 'biggies'—the broad brush strokes of planning your very best retirement—we want to share the secrets of fine-tuning your plan. Several techniques are worth covering in this last chapter—techniques that might not apply to everyone, but for some will turn out to be virtual gold mines of strategic knowledge. Of course, your financial advisor will help you decide if these fine-tuning strategies make sense for your specific situation.

Tax Planning and Tax Projection Tools

Okay, let's shift for a moment to the year you actually retire. That represents a significant milepost in terms of you and the IRS.

When you decide to begin taking disbursements (i.e., payments to you) out of your retirement money, it's important to determine which monies come out of tax-deferred dollars (401[k], IRA's, and the like—qualified funds), and which monies come out of investments that you've already paid tax on (non-qualified, such as individual stocks and mutual funds). There is some strategy involved here. Previous to 1986, the theory was, "defer, defer, defer those taxes!" Financial advisors argued that you should use first what you've already paid taxes on, and leave the deferred money alone for as long as possible. But lately that thinking has changed. What's happened is that people are living longer, so they are eventually going to get to a point where they need to use those deferred dollars.

Let's say, for example, you have $800,000 of assets earmarked for retirement. Of this money, $200,000 is invested in taxable accounts. The other $600,000 is money you've never paid tax on, money socked away in your 401(k) or IRA or other retirement plans. So every penny you take out of the $600,000 is going to be taxed at ordinary income rates, just as if you were still working—and thus still paying income taxes as you earn the money. The thinking behind letting that money grow, unencumbered by income taxes during your working years, is that someday, when you retire, you may be in a smaller income tax bracket, and you could wind up paying less tax on it than if you had paid in earlier years.

The trick to making your money last all the way through retirement is the blending of these two pots of money. It's all about controlling taxes. Generally speaking, at the time of this writing, the five federal income tax brackets are 15%, 28%, 31%, 36% and 39.6%.

Let's say that during your working years you were in the top bracket, 39.6%. If we blend the withdrawals from the two pots just right, we can take advantage of the lower tax brackets. This will minimize the taxes you owe over time. Let's say you retire with $1 million in your 401(k). If you took that entire $1 million out in one year, you would owe the 39.6% federal income tax, plus the highest state tax—let's say 4% for ease of illustration—for a whopping total of almost 44% tax! If you don't do some tax planning in this bad-news scenario, you would owe approximately $440,000 in taxes. So your $1 million isn't worth $1 million, but only about $560,000. That hurts.

Good tax planning would dictate that you

never take out all the money in one year. We can blend the withdrawals so you don't go into those higher tax brackets. This idea of blending is fascinating and complex. The core idea is simple, but there are many variables that enter into the equation in real life. That's why you need a financial advisor to help you.

Estate Planning: Help for Today and Tomorrow

There's a TV commercial running these days that begins with the riveting statement, "Up to two-thirds of your estate could go to the government." Shock journalism? Propaganda—designed to scare folks—not based in reality?

Hardly. If your estate is large enough, and if you haven't taken certain measures to protect assets over the personal exclusion amount, the tax man could indeed get such an ugly chunk of what you had planned on leaving to your children and grandchildren. And even though you'll be dead and won't feel the pain, rest assured that the shock to your heirs will be severe indeed.

But it need not happen; there are perfectly legal and smart ways to make sure that Uncle Sam gets only his bare minimum, and that your heirs—and your favorite charities, if you like—benefit from your hard work, thrift, and smart planning.

If you die with more than the exclusion amount listed in the chart below, your family is going to run into some very heavy estate taxes, which can be as high as 55%. (At the time of this writing, Congress was considering repeal of the so-called death tax, but for now, this chart gives you an idea of the law as it exists in this area.)

Federal Gift & Estate Tax Exclusion

Tax Year	Exemption Equivalent
2001	$675,000
2002	$700,000
2003	$700,000
2004	$850,000
2005	$950,000
2006	$1,000,000

Federal Unified Gift & Estate Tax Rates

Amount of Taxable Transfer	Applicable Marginal Tax Rate
$0 to exemption amount	0%
exemption amount to $750,000	37%
$750,000 to $1,000,000	39%
$1,000,000 to $1,250,000	41%
$1,250,000 to $1,500,000	43%
$1,500,000 to $2,000,000	45%
$2,000,000 to $2,500,000	49%
$2,500,000 to $3,000,000	53%
$3,000,000 +	55%

These tables are simplified and for illustrative purposes only. See a tax professional for more information.

You've heard the old expression that the only two things in life that are 100% sure are death and taxes? Well, we beg to differ. We feel that the estate tax is really a voluntary tax, because there are so many ways to legally avoid paying it. Of course, that's why you need experts on your team. The tragedy is, though, that people don't take advantage of these strategies. They die without wills and without trusts and other tools that can limit the tax man's bite.

Did you know that the IRS allows anyone to give away up to $10,000 annually, tax-free to the recipient? If you know that you have more money than you need to live on, why not give your heirs money while you're alive? It's such a pleasure to do, and the extra satisfaction that the IRS won't get their hands on it is icing on the cake.

Let's say you and your spouse have one child and two grandchildren. You could give each of them $10,000 a year; plus, your spouse could give each of them $10,000 per year, too. So that's $60,000 a year you can jointly gift, tax-free to the recipients, so that upon your demise *all* that money goes to your heirs, without the diluting effect of the death tax.

Another way to leverage this federal gifting provision in favor of your family is to set up an irrevocable life insurance trust. The premiums for the insurance in the trust are paid through gifts to the beneficiaries. An entire book could be written on this topic, so our purpose here is just to let you know it exists.

People often gift the wrong assets. This usually happens because they don't go to an estate tax attorney or a financial advisor, they just plunge ahead and gift various kinds of assets on their own. But there are pitfalls they don't know about until it's too late—and their poor grandchildren are stuck with a nasty surprise: a monstrous tax bill.

For example, let's look at the question of whether you should gift cash or stocks before, or after, you die. This is a rather complicated situation that your financial advisor can explain fully when you sit face-to-face with him, but here are the highlights. If Grandpa decides to gift stocks before he dies, vs. after he dies, through his will, the grandchild might think it's nifty, but the question of capital gains rears its ugly head. If Grandpa has paid, say, $10,000 for his IBM stock decades ago and now it's worth $1 million, it sounds good on the surface. But there's a hidden, ticking time bomb in there.

The grandchild assumes the tax basis for his grandfather. When he sells the stock for $1 million, he now incurs a capital gains tax of 20% on the amount that the value increased. So 20% of the growth, $990,000, is a shocking $198,000, which Junior will have to fork over when he files that year's taxes. That can hurt.

In contrast, if Grandpa has willed this stock to Junior through his estate, there would have been a 'step up' in tax basis, and no tax would have been due if the stock had been sold immediately. Suffice it to say that you need to get expert advice from your financial advisor on these types of questions.

Putting Trusts to Work for You

At this point in your life, you may want to use a living trust, and coordinate your will and titling of your assets to the trust, in order to minimize taxes upon your death. Your attorney and financial advisor can help you with these; there are many advantages of living trusts and more complex types of estate planning vehicles, such as the charitable remainder trust (CRT).

Living trusts will allow assets to pass to heirs without the costs of probate. Other trusts can even save on estate taxes. Charitable remainder trusts can be a great vehicle for turning highly appreciated, non-income-producing assets into a stream of income with minor tax ramifications. Since this is a complex subject, your financial advisor can explain it more fully than we'll go into here.

Using Insurance Wisely

Life insurance—in fact any kind of insurance—is simply a way of managing risk. You can manage the risk of your dying (and its impact on those you leave behind) through life insurance, just as you manage the risk of having your car stolen through automobile insurance.

Some of you have non-liquid assets: a business, investment real estate, or commercial properties. Are you sure you have the right kind of umbrella liability insurance in place so that if you get sued, your assets won't be taken away from you to satisfy a judgment against you? When we were growing up, we all joked about the likelihood of people wanting to sue us for a million dollars—but when you grow up and actually *have* $1 million or more, and they sue you, it's not so funny anymore.

Regular life insurance can benefit your spouse or your children—or your trust. But life insurance for an elderly person can be very expensive. An alternative may be second-to-die insurance. Second-to-die insurance is a special kind of life insurance that pays upon the death of the second person named in the policy (e.g., your spouse), so it is much less expensive than ordinary life insurance, since it doesn't have to pay as early as a regular policy.

There are other types of insurance you may need to consider, and your financial advisor can help you think through the pros and cons of each. One of these is long-term health care insurance for yourself and your spouse. This type of insurance pays for costly nursing home expenses, which can drag on for many years, and which can often eat up an entire estate.

Here's a thought: What about buying this type of insurance for your own parents? They may be healthy now, but if they don't have long-term health care insurance, perhaps you should be looking for a few thousand dollars a year to buy it for them. That could save you *up to $80,000 a year* in long-term care facility expenses if your parents should need it. God willing, they won't, but you need to be prepared for the worst-case scenario.

Pension Enhancement Strategies

Another kind of situation you need to consider is how you take the disbursement from your company pension plan when you actually do retire: in a lump sum, or in payments over time.

In general, we recommend that you take the largest amount you can, in a lump sum. That way, you can put it in the hands of competent financial professional to make it grow, grow, grow.

It may be that you are not even given the option to take a lump-sum distribution of your company pension plan when you are ready to retire. Many companies believe that if they let their employees take a lump sum, they'll squander it. Therefore they don't even give them that option. The employee will usually then choose between several different options in taking a monthly pension.

Option #1 might be this: A retiring employee may take a certain amount of income per month based on life expectancy, and upon his death, his spouse receives nothing.

Option #2 might be this: He may take a little less than the amount in option #1, but with the stipulation that upon his death, his spouse receives the same amount until she dies.

In option #3, he may take an amount somewhere between options #1 and #2; while stipulating that in case of his death, his spouse will get half of what he would have received had he lived. Consider this example:

Option #1. Employee gets $2,200/mo. upon retirement and upon his death, spouse gets $0

Option #2. Employee gets $1,500/mo., and upon his death, spouse gets $1,500/mo. until she dies

Option #3. Employee gets $2,000/mo., and upon his death, spouse gets $1,000/mo. until she dies

Most employees choose option #2 because they don't want to leave their spouse with nothing. But you can enhance your pension and make it work better for you. A way to accomplish this may be to protect your spouse through life insurance, and choose option #1 instead of choosing option #2. It's a purely mathematical decision. You want to do whichever one costs you less in the long run.

Let's flesh this out: say that Joe worked 20 years for General Motors and retires at age 62. He could choose to draw a pension of say, $2,200 a month for the rest of his life. But if Joe dies at age 63, just one year into his golden years, his wife gets nothing. So Joe decides that's not the way to go.

Joe may decide to take only $2,000 a month for the rest of his life, and then if he dies, his wife will get half of that, or $1,000 a month the rest of her life. But option #3 doesn't please Joe either, because he feels that $1,000 a month is a measly amount. He doesn't want to do that to her.

So Joe chooses option #2: he draws $1,500 a month for the rest of his life, and if he dies, his wife continues to get $1,500 a month for the rest of her life. Most people choose this option purely on the basis of raw emotion. But in reality, there is a better way to solve the problem; a way that will save Joe money *and* make both of them feel a whole lot better, too. This is where a good financial advisor can make all the difference in the world.

Between options #1 and #2, the difference between the employee's monthly disbursement (between $2,200 and $1,500) is $700 per month. So in option #2, the guaranteed lifetime income for his wife (assuming she lives to a ripe old age) is costing Joe big-time: $8,400 a year (12 mo.s x $700 = $8,400) in lost income! Over 10 years' time, that's $84,000, not including any earnings on that money! That's not good.

If Joe chooses option #2 anyway and his wife dies first, he's still losing that $8,400 a year (almost $100,000 over 12 years; ouch!) because he cannot reverse his decision, in most cases.

Now let's follow this interesting case study a bit further. Let's assume Joe's wife Mary is 65, with a life expectancy of an additional 30 years, and she could get a CD at 7%. A good financial advisor could tell you that Mary would need $300,000 to generate $1,500 a month for the rest of her life. If Joe could purchase a $300,000 life insurance policy for less than $8,400 a year, Joe and Mary would both be better off. Joe and Mary would have more money to spend during their lifetime and, if something were to happen to Joe, Mary would be covered. Conversely, if Mary were to die, Joe could change the beneficiary on the life insurance to his children, or opt to cancel the policy.

Thus we have Joe take option #1 and we buy a $300,000 life insurance policy for his wife, instead of losing $8,400 per year. We've just saved Joe a pile of dough, and Mary will be just as well off when and if Joe dies before she does.

Now, in all likelihood, Joe's company is not going to mention this technique to Joe, nor give him any advice on his choice among the first three. A word of caution: Some companies may not provide health care coverage for the spouse in option #1 or #2, but they do in option #3; thus forcing Joe to take option #3, because this saves *them* money. In option #3 they pay out the least amount of money to Joe *and* his wife.

In most cases, if the company offers a lump-sum disbursement, take it. Because in our experience, 99% of the time, a lump sum managed by a professional will give a person more money for a longer period of time than any of the other options. In other situations—such as if an employee has no investment experience and refuses to hire a professional to help— a lump sum may not work because people lose sleep, get frustrated, and are afraid of managing money. In that case, it's not worth it. For every person and every company, the correct choice may be different.

Toys

People say the only difference between men

and boys is the price of their toys. There's some truth in that, but it also applies to women! Whether it's buying boats or fast cars, redecorating the entire house, or buying a cozy cottage up north on the lake, this area deserves some general guidance, too. We believe in having some fun with your money, if you can afford it—all budgetary discipline and saying "no" to your desires can make for some dullness after awhile if it's not spiced up with appropriate bits of fun.

So in your planning, decide what amount you can reasonably afford for lifestyle enhancements. If you can afford it, what's wrong with buying a $10,000 Harley-Davidson motorcycle? And what's wrong with buying a cute little A-frame in a remote Rocky Mountain valley for $90,000, if you can swing it? The key is not doing such things on an impulse basis, but rather, budgeting for them, sticking to your plan, and then enjoying them!

One last bit of advice: don't finance your toys. Pay cash.

Do What Retirement Planners Do

We look very closely at each person we hire to work in our firm and ask ourselves, *Is this the type of professional we want to work on our own retirement plan someday?* Because even we, as retirement planning professionals, realize that it's not a good idea to go it alone. Even we want the benefits of the emotional distance that hiring someone else to help manage our money can bring. Even we know that bringing in more expertise than we have individually will be spectacularly beneficial as we march toward our own golden years.

Don't do any less for yourself—get the best help you can find, and work together with a competent retirement financial professional on attaining your retirement dreams. It just makes sense to link up with someone who has specific training, skills, and the objectivity to help you make the right strategic moves for your future.

And there is one more very special reason: you deserve it.

EPILOGUE

You can't just let retirement *happen*. You can't be merely reactive in this most important of life's tasks; you must become proactive. That's why we've written this book.

Lifestyle choices have much more impact on a successful retirement than do earnings. This runs counter to the impressions we pick up from our culture, where we figure we have to become an overnight dot-com millionaire to be able to afford to retire someday. The plodding path of a loyal employee who worked for 40+ years seems to be too slow to get much of anywhere, we think.

Yet it's all a matter of perspective. For example, one morning a young hot-shot executive came into our offices and, after working some preliminary numbers, asked his financial advisor, with fear and desperation in his voice, "How am I going to live on

$18,000 a month in retirement?" (He was accustomed to making in the realm of $30,000 per month.)

In contrast, the next day another client came in, a single mom making $35,000 a year and putting two kids through college. She wanted our help to shape her already modest lifestyle and somewhat meager savings into a healthy retirement plan. After some planning sessions and quite a few years of working her plan, she was able to retire comfortably and is quite happy, the grandmother of six.

See the difference? Success in retirement is all about your mental attitude and lifestyle decisions.

One of our financial advisors once spoke to a group of high school kids about financial planning. One of them asked him for a definition of success. Any conventional definition of success he would have given those kids on first thought would have excluded many of them; chances were slim that they would grow up to be millionaires. Luckily he paused and thought further about his answer, since he was on the verge of telling them that they probably wouldn't be successful!

Fortunately what came out of his mouth was something different, and it just flowed. He will always remember it. He told that high school class that the best definition of success is "having a plan and then taking the first step of that plan."

He continued, "If you want to go to college and become a doctor—that's your plan. Passing your biochemistry test next week is the first step in that plan. Work on that today and, chances are, your tomorrows will turn out just fine."

The same goes for retirement. If you want to retire successfully, all it takes is a plan—and then, taking that very first step.

HELPFUL
RESOURCES

❖ First and foremost, of course, see our web site, <www.ncafinancial.com>.

❖ To select a qualified financial planning professional in your area, contact the Financial Planning Association at 1-800-322-4237. You may also do a search online at <www.fpanet.org>.

❖ The U.S. Securities & Exchange Commission ("the investor's advocate") offers a list of questions you should ask about your investments and what to do if you run into problems. See this at <www.sec.gov/consumer/askqinv.htm>.

❖ Learn about the disciplinary history of any bro-

kerage firm and sales representatives by calling
1-800-289-9999. This is a toll-free hotline oper-
ated by the National Association of Securities
Dealers, Inc. (NASD). See <www.nasdr.com>.

ORDERING THIS BOOK

If you are interested in obtaining additional copies of this book or ordering them in bulk, please contact Kevin Myeroff or Kelly Russell by telephone at (440) 473-1115 or by e-mail at kmyeroff@ncafinancial.com